JAN **0 9** 2020

WHITE FANG AND THE GOLDEN BEAR

A FATHER-AND-SON JOURNEY ON THE GOLF COURSE AND BEYOND

JOE WESSEL
WITH BILL CHASTAIN

Foreword by Jack Nicklaus

Skyhorse Publishing

This book is dedicated to Louis Joseph Wessel—Renaissance Man, Navy Man, Best Friend, Loving Father, and Leader of the Wessel Band!

Skyhorse Publishing books may be purchased in bulk at special discounts for sales promotion, corporate gifts, fund-raising, or educational purposes. Special editions can also be created to specifications. For details, contact the Special Sales Department, Skyhorse Publishing, 307 West 36th Street, 11th Floor, New York, NY 10018 or info@skyhorsepublishing.com.

Skyhorse® and Skyhorse Publishing® are registered trademarks of Skyhorse Publishing, Inc.®, a Delaware corporation.

Visit our website at www.skyhorsepublishing.com.

10 9 8 7 6 5 4 3 2 1

Library of Congress Cataloging-in-Publication Data is available on file.

Cover design by Qualcom Designs
Cover photo credit: iStock

ISBN: 978-1-5107-4016-7
Ebook ISBN 978-15107-4017-4

Printed in the United States of America

Contents

Foreword
by Jack Nicklaus

My father was my best friend. I know how lucky I was to have had a special relationship with him.

I think my sister got a little bit of the short end of that deal. That didn't mean he loved her any less. But I was the apple of Dad's eye, and he spent a ton of time with me. He introduced me to every sport. We threw the ball together. We shot baskets together. We kicked the football together. We played golf together. We hit tennis balls together. Whatever, that's what we did.

Dad taught me a lot of things. There was a right way to do things. Like you wanted to be a good sport. If you lost, it wasn't the end of the world. You have to deal with whatever hand you're dealt. And, you kept your word. Your word is your bond. He also taught me how a father was supposed to act, so I tried to do the same thing with all of my kids. He taught me to introduce my kids to things and let them make up their own minds. I didn't want any of my kids to play golf just because I wanted them to play golf. I wanted them to play golf if *they* wanted to play golf. I'd introduce them to the game, but I didn't actually try to encourage them too much. I thought it was pretty difficult being my son from that standpoint. And if they ended up wanting to play, then that would be a great choice on their part. Well, it turned out that three of the four boys became golf pros. Steve did not. But Steve was almost as good a golfer as the other three. It made me very happy that my sons wanted to play, just as my dad was happy that I enjoyed the sport on my own terms.

Dad was a great athlete. He'd even played pro football for the old Portsmouth Spartans, who are now the Detroit Lions. I didn't know it at the time, but Dad had wanted me to play football, too. You know, I quit football, and he never told me he was disappointed. He just supported what I wanted to do. And so that's sort of what I did with my guys.

Obviously, Dad was a heavy influence in my life. He passed away far too early, at 56 of pancreatic cancer. He missed a great part of my career. But he got to see probably seven or eight major championships. I think about him every day.

A component of this book originated from the fact that one of my sons gave something away. My kids used to give all my stuff away. And that's ok.

I had obtained one autograph during my childhood, that of Harvey Haddix. Most remember him as the guy who pitched a perfect game for the Pittsburgh Pirates before losing the game in extra innings. When Harvey played for the Columbus Redbirds, I got his autograph on a baseball. I was 6 or 7 years old. I had kept that ball on my dresser my entire life. Then one day, I came home from a trip, and the baseball wasn't on my dresser. I wondered what happened until my son Steve, who was about 15 at the time, came in and said, "Oh Dad, our ball went in the lake, so we used this one." He showed me the Haddix ball, and, of course, it was a mess. The autograph was gone. But that's what kids do."

Funny that White Fang would be one of the items he'd give away years later.

Obviously, a putter's probably the most important club in your bag. You really have to have a good feel for your putter. If you're not comfortable with what you're using, you're out of luck. You have to have confidence in what you've got. If you don't have confidence in it, you're not going to use it very well. I had that one putter I used for years, a George Low Wizard heel-shafted putter. I won fifteen of my majors with it. But there were times when all of a sudden it felt different. I wasn't making any putts, so I'd put it down and putt with something else and have success. White Fang became one of those alternative putters.

White Fang was a Bull's Eye putter painted white. When I looked at it, it gave me a different look. I putted well with it, and I gained confidence from using it, even won a major using it, the 1967 U.S. Open at Baltusrol. You're not going to win if you don't have any confidence.

I met Joe Wessel when he roomed with Steve at Florida State. They both played football, so they spent a little bit of time together and became good friends. Joe ended up playing a little bit of golf, so they shared some time from that side, too. Occasionally, I'd see Joe when I went to Tallahassee for games. I'd always liked him, and when he returned White Fang to me, I liked him even more.

Getting White Fang back helped to facilitate a memorable outing. Joe Wessel had a special relationship with his father, a relationship that is the heart of this book. Being able to play a small part in their life together was something that brought me pure joy. I think that was a special day for Joe, and a special day for his dad. I hope you enjoy Joe's account, as told by Bill Chastain, as much as I enjoyed partaking in it.

Prologue

PRIOR TO MY FATHER'S DEATH, every time we played a round of golf together, we'd sit down afterward, and inevitably, somebody would want me to cue up the White Fang story. "Tell it, Joe. It's the best golf story ever."

Something similar occurred inside the Men's Grill at the Palma Ceia Golf and Country Club in Tampa. I sat swapping stories with my friend Doug Shields, when Bill Chastain stopped by our table. Doug introduced us and told me he was a writer. Doug calls everyone "Coach" and has a way with words, so he yelled out, "Coach, tell Bill the White Fang story! Bill, you won't believe this story." I told him the story, and that marked the beginning of this book's journey.

Dad had died a couple of months earlier. The sting of his death remained fresh. I missed him so badly that I physically hurt. My neighbor Ralph Barber had been pushing me to write a book, so I asked Bill if he might be interested in collaborating with me. The next day, Bill got back to me after he'd researched the White Fang story. Several articles had been written about how Jack Nicklaus got reunited with his beloved putter, White Fang, but those stories missed the larger backstory, which dealt with a special father-son relationship. Once I told Bill more about my father and our unique relationship—along with some details from my life—we agreed to work on this book.

I first met Jack in Tallahassee, Florida, where his son Steve and I were college roommates. Steve and I played football for Florida State University. During that time, I learned that Jack cared about relationships and understood that relationships were more important than anything else. Relationships were about getting along and about engaging other people. Observing Jack made me think of my father's work with Alcoholics Anonymous and how he guided other people. That's what defines true servant leadership.

In the years that would follow, when I became a husband and a father, how I saw Jack as a father meant even more to me. When I looked back and heard stories about what happened to Jack's father and how he felt about his family, everything resonated with me. There were many similarities between my own father and Jack.

Jack plays a unique role in this story. He ultimately punched the Augusta lottery ticket for my father and me. With approximately 29 million golfers in the United States and in Europe, there's no telling what the odds were for any golfer to ever have the good fortune of playing a round of golf at Augusta National, home of The Masters. The place ranks among the top golf courses in the world, and with that rank comes exclusivity. Limited numbers of rounds on those pristine grounds are allowed yearly by its own members. Couple the odds of getting to play a round at Augusta with the odds of getting to play Augusta with Jack Nicklaus—a six-time winner of The Masters tournament—and the odds become astronomical.

However, before the story of how we got to Augusta unfolds, we must uncover another story, one that should echo in the heart of any son or daughter who ever enjoyed a special relationship with his or her father.

I've always felt that the life I lead reflects my dreams and my passion. My father had always enjoyed the fact that I had an affinity for sports, and ultimately, for coaching. He'd followed his passion to entertain and sing on Broadway, and he wanted me to experience similar joy. And I did, from growing up around the Miami Dolphins of the 1970s and early 1980s, to playing college football at Florida State University and eventually coaching in the college and professional ranks. Dreams do come true, and sometimes in the strangest of ways.

My father gave me the ultimate lesson on how to be a leader through the discipline he dispatched and by the way he lived his life. Watching him and listening to him gave me an understanding of passion and hard work. You have to be an example to the people you lead. I have strived for that in my coaching career, in my business life, and in my personal life.

Dad was a regional sales manager for McCormick & Company, but I think he always fell back on his Navy experience from World War II, where he learned about the hierarchy of leadership and being a stickler about details—doing things right.

Along the way, I was exposed to many different coaches, including Don Shula, Bill Arnsparger, Howard Schnellenberger, Bobby Bowden, Jack Stanton, Mickey Andrews, Lou Holtz, and countless others. Coaching is all about getting people to buy into a philosophy, then getting them to execute the things that are needed for success, some of which they never thought possible. Both of my parents provided a foundation for that way of thinking. My mother taught English and always strived to have us speak correctly. You said you were "doing well." You didn't say you were "doing good." That's what we parents do, because we want our kids to be better than we were.

Once I got out of football and into business, the bells started going off when others would comment about the people I have met, the places I have been to, and the experiences that have formed and guided my life. I can look back and say they've all helped to form the person I am. No person is more responsible for who I am than my father, Louis Joseph Wessel.

CHAPTER 1

Anticipation
October 2003

SITTING ON THE BACK PORCH of Firestone Cabin at Augusta National, my mind raced. I reflected on my life and considered the possibilities of the next day.

I had a downhill view through the pine trees of the No. 10 fairway thanks to a bright moon. Temperatures were in the 50s, and the wind whistled through the pines. The forecast for the next day was clear and in the 60s. Perfect golf weather.

Although the azaleas weren't blooming in the fall, the visualization of a full accompaniment of the signature flowers sat in my brain, just not in my nose. I'd played in baseball stadiums and I'd coached and played in football stadiums, but golf is a different sport altogether. When you play a course, you can go out and do exactly what the pro did, a month after or a day after he finished a tournament. Golf has that capability. And you can play the exalted venues where legends are formed or dismantled. Augusta National is such a venue.

Firestone Cabin sat in the middle of a semicircle of newer cabins at Augusta National. The famed Butler Cabin sits off the 10th tee near the 9th green. Everybody in the cabin slept that night except me. Among those sleeping were my father; my college roommate, Steve Nicklaus; and Jack Nicklaus—the Golden Bear, who happened to be Steve's father.

I felt as though I'd experienced a reversal of roles, putting my seventy-seven-year-old father to bed like I'd tucked in my kids before treating them to the circus the following day.

Three years earlier, a friend offered me tickets for a practice round at The Masters. I accepted and brought my father with me. We drove from Tampa and back the same day. What an experience! Dad remained in a state of awe watching the practice round and some of the par-3 tournament. We walked a lot; he'd been in good shape then, and the fibrosis hadn't taken its toll yet. Dad commented at one point, "Man, the TV doesn't do this place justice." He couldn't believe the course's elevations. Augusta National's beauty captured him, sending him back to his days of tending to his orchids on the side of the house.

Right in his wheelhouse.

No doubt, Dad walked off the course that day thinking he'd never see the place again, much less ever have an opportunity to play the course. Yet now I found myself, perched on the brink of stepping inside the ropes to play Augusta National, and privy to doing so with my father, my college roommate, and the golfer hailed as the best to ever play the game. How would I handle the treacherous greens? Amen Corner? I wanted morning to arrive. I wanted to tee off. I wanted to putt on the immaculate greens. I just didn't want the night to end.

White Fang would be picking up the check.

Had that magical putter not brought comfort to Nicklaus for a fleeting moment during his storied career, my Augusta experience would never have come to fruition.

CHAPTER 2

Louis Joseph Wessel

HURRICANE SEASON IN THE ATLANTIC proved to be particularly feisty in the summer of 1926. When you lived in Miami Beach like my grandparents, Louis and Esther Wessel, you had to pay attention to such things.

On July 22, 1926, the National Weather Service reported the first hurricane of the season. Reports of another tropical depression forming on July 29 prompted a decision by my pregnant grandmother to travel by train to Dubuque, Iowa. She could have her baby surrounded by a large Bertsch clan, thousands of miles from the possibility of hurricane devastation.

The previous year, my grandparents had lost their first, Patrick, due to complications from the birth. Given the fact the only hospital near where they lived was inland, along with the lingering heartbreak from the loss of Patrick, the precautions they took were understandable.

On August 14, 1926, Louis Joseph Wessel came into the world in a hospital in Dubuque. The decision to temporarily relocate proved to be a wise one. Eleven tropical storms took place in, or around, the Atlantic that year. Among those, the "Great Miami Hurricane" arrived on September 18.

The nastiest part of that historic storm saw Miami Beach get hit with a ten-foot storm surge that sent water from the Atlantic Ocean as far as the City of Miami, leaving several city blocks covered by water. According to the Red Cross, 372 people died in the storm and another 6,000 were injured. The estimated cost from the damages inflicted amounted to $105 million, according to the National Weather Service, which notes that in today's dollars, damages from that storm would equate to approximately $164 billion.

Two months after my grandmother had given birth, the weather in the Atlantic settled, and she boarded a train to Miami Beach to be reunited with my grandfather. It was there that they would raise my father, along with the other nine children that followed. My grandmother gave birth to ten kids in twelve years, including one set of twins.

My grandfather worked in the construction business, a less than ideal business after the Depression hit. Difficult circumstances, both physical and economic, followed. Though my grandparents weren't poor, they were far from wealthy. They made do with little spending money.

Dad always described my grandmother as a queen, noting that everybody always talked about her gregarious nature and generosity. Despite the family's circumstances and tight living conditions, my grandmother would insist that they could find room for a visitor if he or she needed to stay overnight. Somehow, she would manage to find a place for them to sleep while also finding enough food to feed them.

Being the oldest of ten, with five brothers and four sisters, Dad had the platform to become a leader, a counselor, a big brother, and a friend to his siblings. The three-bedroom house in which they lived had one bathroom and no air conditioning. A survival-of-the-fittest climate existed, teaching the kids that the early riser got the better shoes—and the most food. Not having money to go to the movies or other forms of entertainment, Dad became a tinkerer, developing a natural curiosity about how things worked and how to fix them. My grandmother knew how to cook circles around most, and she could play the piano. No doubt, those skills rubbed off on Dad, as did her love of music. Eventually, that love would weave itself into every part of his life, and mine.

Dad attended St. Patrick's School in Miami Beach. St. Patrick's, and the church to which it was attached, were built in the aftermath of the "Great Miami Hurricane." My grandfather, Louis, helped build the church along with the school gymnasium. Attending the Catholic school hardly filled Dad's vision of heaven. Instead, the beach represented his idea of the Promise Land. Any time spent in the sand and salt water was time well spent—particularly when skipping school. Said excursions would usually involve fishing or diving in the Atlantic Ocean. At times, he would combine the two activities to spearfish for grouper and snapper off Miami Beach. Despite being anything but wealthy, Dad also was introduced to golf in his early years, receiving instruction from Denny Rouse, one of the first-known golf professionals in Normandy Isle.

During Dad's freshman and sophomore years in high school, he worked part-time at a gas station. Being around cars and engines pleased him.

Thanks to World War II, he never graduated from St. Patrick's.

The Japanese attacked Pearl Harbor on December 7, 1941. Like many Americans, Dad heard about the attack via the radio. Subsequent reports of the activities that followed, along with the wave of patriotism in the country, captured his attention.

My grandfather's work often put him in different areas where bridges and other projects were being constructed. That left doling out much of the discipline to my grandmother and the St. Patrick's nuns and priests.

Dad had worn down the nuns, who had tired of tracking him

down and trying to haul him back to school. Finally, my grand-mother issued the ultimatum: "Look, you're either going to stay in school, or you're going to the war."

Music to Dad's ears.

On February 27, 1942, Dad chose the war. Despite being just fifteen, he had already been thinking about joining the war effort. A friend of his, Leo Collins, served on a Navy battleship. Leo filled Dad's ears with tales of the foreign countries he'd visited. Dad's mind drifted and dreamed, bringing thoughts of the ocean, exotic islands, and a lot of girls. And why not? Remember, he lived in a small house with his nine siblings, and meanwhile, his relationships with the Catholic nuns grew more contentious daily. It's no wonder that the Navy looked like an attractive destination, even if combat might be part of the assignment.

Believing that the United States' mainland could be attacked next, countless young and patriotic American men enlisted. I have to agree with Tom Brokaw, who called that generation the "Greatest Generation."

Dad figured he could join even if underaged. He lied when he went with a friend to enlist, telling them he was seventeen. Even with the addition of two years to his alleged age, the Navy informed him he needed to have a signed release from his parents to go anchors aweigh. My grandparents signed off.

Being a father, I can't imagine signing off to allow one of my sons to join the military, particularly at the age of fifteen.

The Navy accepted Dad in February of 1942, and he reported for duty at the end of the month, on February 27, 1942.

CHAPTER 3

Off to War

TODAY, DAD'S CLASSIFICATION WOULD BE known as a VUMS, or Veteran Underage Military Service.

Basic training took place at the Naval Operating Base in Norfolk, Virginia. Because so many men entered the Navy at the same time, there wasn't room for all of them at the facility. Accordingly, training got delayed, as did assignments. Dad had to spend months at Norfolk before the Navy could find a place for him. Many others shared the same experience.

Dad's resistance to discipline added to the difficulty of basic training. When speaking about himself as a young man, he allowed, "I was kind of an independent cuss. But I got through it very well."

Trainees at the facility were assigned to different schools such as aviation school, mechanic school, and radio operator school, to name a few. Those who weren't assigned to one of the schools were immediately assigned to ship duty. Dad fell into the latter category, receiving the classification of apprentice seaman.

Fresh out of boot camp in July of 1942, Dad got assigned aboard a troop carrier, USS *Thomas Stone*, named after a signer of the Declaration of Independence. Two months later, Dad was transferred to USS *Simpson*, a four-stack destroyer from World War I named for Rear Admiral Edward Simpson.

Escort duty in the Atlantic turned out to be the *Simpson*'s mission. The ship would travel up and down the East Coast of the United States, offering submarine patrol and protection for the freighters and troop carriers from Guantanamo Bay to Boston and New York.

While on the *Simpson*, Dad got the news in November of 1942 that the *Thomas Stone* had been torpedoed while on the way to the invasion of Casablanca in North Africa. Fortunately, the troops aboard survived.

Dad was transferred again on December 1, 1942, going from the *Simpson* to New York. Pier 92 operated as a receiving station during the war when the *Queen Mary*, the *Normandie*, and many other big cruise ships docked there and got converted into barracks. Thousands of double-decker beds were installed and became home to over 10,000 sailors.

Getting assigned to New York turned into one of the best experiences of Dad's life.

Menial duties kept him and his fellow sailors busy most mornings, while free time came during most afternoons, enabling them to venture into New York City to entertain themselves. Dad dedicated much of his time to cultivating his interest in music.

Ethel Merman and Irving Berlin starred in the first Broadway show he saw. Sammy Kaye, Glenn Miller, and many of the big bands of that era played in the city. Dad even saw Frank Sinatra perform at the Paramount Theatre. By the time his two months of duty in New York City had run its course, his passion for music had been effectively stoked. For the first time ever, an idea about what he wanted to do in life percolated inside his mind.

Dad was transferred to Little Creek, Virginia, in February of 1943 and got assigned to a newly designed type of a ship, known as an LCI—Landing Craft Infantry. These were lightly armed amphibious assault vessels designed to land troops when they made beachhead assaults. The crew of twenty-three men—nineteen enlisted men and four officers—shipped out on February 6, 1943, in the 135-foot ship, spending twenty-six days navigating the small ship from the Atlantic to the Pacific. It was not exactly easy duty, since the LCI had not been designed to navigate heavy seas. At such times, the vessel could feel like a cork floating in the water. The crew had to get along in the tight quarters, coping with the intense heat while living on a diet consisting primarily of Spam dishes. On the bright side, they had a cook who knew how to make the best cornbread Dad had ever tasted.

Dad advanced from apprentice seaman, to seaman second class, and then to a seaman first class. While serving on the LCI, he renewed his interest in mechanics and went into the "Black Gang" as a motor machinist, learning a lot about the engines that supplied the power that propelled the ship through the water.

Dad helped take care of the engines and saw that they were serviced properly, and he had a battle station, as did everyone on the crew. When general quarters sounded, whether they were in battle or anticipating going into battle, they had to be at their battle stations. For Dad, that meant being the gunner on a 20-millimeter cannon.

Daily duties also included watch duty, a duty everybody on the ship shared, that usually constituted four hours on, four hours off, four hours on, then eight hours off.

On that tiny vessel, they went to Bora Bora, Fiji, Samoa, Noumea, and Sydney before they were to head for Guadalcanal in April of 1943.

The Battle of Guadalcanal began on August 7, 1942, and continued until February 9, 1943. Amphibious warfare had played a large role throughout the battle. Fortunately, the Marines had the island well under control by the time Dad's LCI had been scheduled to arrive, so their ship, and the flotilla in which they traveled, got reassigned to New Guinea, where things were going badly.

At any given time, they traveled as part of a six- to twelve-ship flotilla. They took part in a mission at Buna, which the Army had captured months earlier. Dad's LCI would transport a company of men—normally close to two hundred infantry personnel, from spot A to spot B, where the battle took place. As the boat approached its intended landfall, they would drop a large spiked anchor off the stern several hundred yards away from the beach. They would beach the boat as close to land as possible. The troops would unload on the beach using the ship's bow ramps. After the disembarkation of the troops, they would use the machine pulley that was connected to the anchor to then pull the ship off the beach to return it to the sea.

Over the course of the next year and a half, they made many landings up and down the New Guinea coast before jumping to New Britain, where they transported Marines into battle. They also transported Australian soldiers. On one occasion that included an Australian division that had just departed South Africa, they had engaged the "Desert Fox," German General Erwin Rommel, and his famed tank corps.

Throughout, they conducted a series of leapfrogging exercises. General Douglas MacArthur developed a strategy that would cut off the enemy's supply line by leapfrogging around the enemy rather than fighting through him.

Dad was rotated back to the United States in December of 1944, taking a ship to San Francisco to begin a thirty-day leave.

During that time, he returned to Miami, where he enjoyed getting reacquainted with civilian life. Mostly, he just hung out, having fun with women, going to the dance halls and the USO shows. The Air Force operated a huge training base for officer training schools in Miami Beach. Sailors were welcomed at their activities, so they had a ball. They received hero treatment everywhere they went.

Dad always maintained they weren't heroes, noting, "Those were the guys who didn't come home."

After the thirty days passed, Dad had to report to Cape Bradford, Virginia, near Norfolk, to be reassigned. Once again, he got assigned to an amphibious vessel. You could say the assignment left Dad somewhat south of being a happy camper. This time, he found himself aboard an LST, which carried twice the amount of an LCI. A sailor couldn't do anything about his assignment, so, dutifully, he reported to his new ship in January of 1945.

While the LCI only carried infantry and could carry up to a company, or two hundred men, an LST had a huge open space, with the operation part of the ship on the stern. Tanks, boats, and other amphibious crafts could be transported on an LST, which ran 340 feet long. They only had twenty-four crew members on the LCI. Seventy-four crew members manned the LST, bringing a different environment and making Dad miserable.

Just like the other time Dad shipped out of Virginia, they followed a path that cut through the Panama Canal to the Pacific. A stop at Pearl Harbor afforded them a firsthand look at the devastation from the December 7, 1941, attack. Being a young man, Dad spent most of that two-day stop at the Royal Hawaiian Hotel, because that's where most of the servicemen who went to Hawaii wanted to go.

After the stop in Hawaii, they set sail for the Philippines, arriving shortly after the invasion of the island. They were grateful the island had been secured before their arrival. The Philippines invasion had brought a lot of losses.

They transported men and equipment from city to city in the Philippines before winding up in Manila. Then they transported tanks and armored vehicles to Okinawa. That summer, while leaving Okinawa, they were subjected to the worst series of typhoons that ever affected the US Navy.

Japan is located in the typhoon belt. Typhoons were frequent occurrences that summer and continued to haunt the Navy through November. To grasp how powerful those typhoons could be, USS *Hornet*, an Essex-class carrier that had survived numerous battles at sea, saw the front edge of its flight deck collapse by the force of 138 mph winds. That forced the *Hornet* and its 2,500-man crew to head to California for repairs. Dad's ship survived by making port in Ie Shima, the little island north of Okinawa where Japanese machine gunfire had killed famed war correspondent Ernie Pyle.

Pyle had been killed on April 18, 1945, after coming ashore with the Army's 305th Infantry Regiment of the 77th "Liberty Patch" Division. Dad, like others in the military, thought highly of Pyle, who wasn't shy about going into combat. The monument on Ie Shima that honored Pyle moved Dad accordingly.

While they were on the island, Dad and his entire ship received the news on August 6 and 9 that atom bombs had been dropped on Hiroshima and Nagasaki. News of a Japanese surrender had quickly followed.

The Navy didn't know where to send Dad's ship after the surrender. First, they were directed to Korea, where they unloaded the vehicles aboard. They then sailed to Tientsin, China, which is located on the coast across the Sea of Japan from Sasebo, Japan. Several trips followed where they transported Japanese prisoners of war from China back to their homeland.

In November, Dad was put on a ship headed to San Francisco. From there, he took a five-day train trip to Jacksonville, Florida. After receiving an honorable discharge at Jacksonville Naval Air Station on December 24, 1945, Dad returned to Miami Beach. What a Christmas present!

Dad said of his time in the Navy that it had its ups and downs and though he wouldn't take a million dollars to do it all again, he was happy that he'd served. He stressed that he learned a lot from the experience, which allowed him to explore other parts of the world and taught him how to deal with trying circumstances. Above all, he felt grateful, and fortunate, to have finished his service without incurring an injury, mental or physical.

CHAPTER 4

Home, and Broadway

DAD FOUND HIMSELF IN A situation similar to what hundreds of thousands of men experienced when returning to civilian life after the war. The Navy had been all he'd known from the time he was fifteen until he was nineteen, and he had no idea what he wanted to do for the rest of his life, or even in his immediate future.

He'd already recognized the fact that not having graduated from high school would be a detriment, and he began to address that deficiency before leaving the Navy. Correspondence courses were offered by the Armed Forces Network while he served in the Pacific, and he took advantage of that opportunity. Once he returned to Miami, he went to a local high school that offered a course in how to pass the GED test. After getting his high school diploma out of the way, Dad's thoughts turned to music. My grandmother had music in her blood. She could play the piano by ear. Not until Dad returned home from World War II did he discover that he, too, had a passion for music. That love of music prompted him to enroll at the University of Miami via the G.I. Bill, and he graduated with a liberal arts degree with a major in music.

Dad had a tenor voice. The tenor is not the extreme high range of a male voice, but it is a high range. A "bass" voice registers as the deep voice, with "baritone" coming in the middle of the two. Examples of modern-day tenors are Luciano Pavarotti and Placido Domingo. Maybe that's why Dad loved Pavarotti.

Shooting for the moon, Dad saw a musical career on Broadway as the next logical adventure of his life. Ignoring the staggering odds against success on the grandest of stages, he again left Miami Beach and headed to New York City, where he had felt the pulse of the big city and had so enjoyed the music and Broadway shows.

During his three years in the Big Apple, he performed in Broadway musicals, road shows, and summer stock. *Brigadoon*, *Kiss Me Kate*, *Carousel*, and *Oklahoma*, were just some of the numerous shows in which he participated.

Performing on Broadway had parallels to being an athlete. Broadway actors and actresses did nine shows a week, with two matinees. You had to be in great shape to physically adhere to such a schedule. And when the lights came on, you had to set aside any nerves and perform. I think it's a fair comparison.

Young, single, and full of life, Dad loved his time on Broadway, even if he had to supplement his income by working as a chef.

In the end, Dad had talent, but he recognized that the odds were stacked against him to succeed in the tough entertainment business. Even those more talented than he failed. Chasing hard the Broadway dream finally drove home the realization to him that he hadn't made a lucrative career choice. He always said of his days on Broadway, "I did a lot more cooking than I did singing!" Looking to make a change and earn more money, he moved back to Miami Beach, where he could enjoy the ocean, the beach, and his family.

Dad's return to Miami Beach also signaled the beginning of his career as a piano bar singer. He became the Frank Sinatra of Miami Beach, performing in the hotel lounges and The Surfside Bandshell. Piano bars were popular in the 1950s and 1960s during the Rat Pack's heyday, and the influences of Sinatra, Dean Martin, and Sammy Davis were undeniable. All of the hotels at the beach at that time had lounges. Performers like Dad were usually accompanied by piano players. A blind man, Hal Di Ciccio, became Dad's favorite pianist, and they formed a duo.

Singing in lounges, Dad stayed true to his tenor voice, though he imitated a lot of the popular singers of the day. And, obviously, many of his selections were influenced by Broadway.

Dad's return to Miami Beach also set the stage for him to meet my mother.

Two of Dad's sisters, Margaret and Rita, attended St. Patrick's also, and they played sports. In their high school days, they played against this girl from the other side of the tracks at St. Mary's. Her name: Marjorie Parker.

Their love of sports and basketball in particular continued after their college days, and it paired them up in a local basketball league. One night, Dad had nothing to do, and as a good brother would do, he went to watch his sisters play. Afterward, he asked his sisters to help him meet the blonde woman everyone called "Marge."

Dad's sisters coaxed Marge into dressing up and going with them to a speakeasy at Normandy Isle in Miami Beach. They knew Dad would be performing that night. Dad became instantly smitten after being introduced to Marge. Anybody in the audience would have surmised as much by observing how he sang to her most of that night. They began to date, and they were married on January 4, 1957.

Kids followed.

My older sister, Margie, came in 1959. I was born in 1962. And my younger sister, Ann Marie, came in 1970.

Dad continued to sing even after he had a family, balancing piano bars with a career as the regional sales manager for Nestlé followed by a thirty-plus-year career with McCormick & Co., which earned him the nickname "Spicey Joe." "Spicy Joe" worked well with my nickname, "Tiger Joe," which I acquired early in my childhood, when Esso gas stations came up with the slogan "Put a Tiger in Your Tank!" One of their promotions called for Esso stations to hand out a stuffed tiger if you filled up your gas tank. Once Dad filled up, I got the tiger. I guess I never parted with the stuffed animal, and that's how I got the nickname "Tiger Joe."

Dad called on hotels and restaurants throughout the southern half of Florida. The job put him on the road a lot. In the summer, we'd go with him for a week or two on his tours. When he covered Orlando, the Ramada Inn in Altamonte Springs became one of our yearly stops. Naples was also one of our tour stops at the Kings Crown Inn on Vanderbilt Beach.

Dad's travel limited his family time. He wanted to maximize that time whenever possible and often mixed his love of the outdoors with his duties as a father helping to raise his kids. We did a lot of boating, fishing, spear fishing, water skiing, and our favorite, diving for lobster.

Tinkering with things remained a consistent practice of his. He may not have been a licensed boat-motor mechanic, but what he learned in the war gave him enough knowledge to be dangerous. He faked the rest of it. Mechanical problems with the boat stranded us out in the Atlantic on many occasions. Usually, he could fix the problem, and we'd manage to get home. Other times, he couldn't. When that happened, we'd have to wait around for somebody to tow us in. Sea Tow didn't exist back then.

You always got the sense Dad knew what he was doing and that he would get us home safely. I'd heard all the stories on the docks about bad things happening to boaters. In my mind, those stories happened to other people, not us. I never realized how dangerous our boating excursions were, because I had no reference. I only knew that Dad had served in the Navy. That qualified him to get us out of anything we could get into. Besides that, Dad was Dad. He'd probably get thrown in jail these days for taking out an eight- and ten-year-old some thirty-five miles from the coast on a boat with a single engine Evinrude 115, no cell phone, and a two-wave radio that rarely worked. But that's what he did. He was a true sportsman. He loved the water, and we loved being out there with him.

Dad's tinkering wasn't limited to mechanical issues. He'd tinker around the house, too, fixing pipes, toilets, or anything that happened to be broken. I don't know if he faked his way through some of those projects or if he simply knew how to fix everything. He came off as the Home Depot man long before Home Depot. Once Home Depot did come about, Dad found a home away from home.

Music always played in our house. I never knew a day when the turntable wasn't running. It didn't matter if we were working or just sitting around—Broadway show tunes blared around the clock. *My Fair Lady, Camelot, Oliver*—you name a show, and he probably cued it up on that old Hi-Fi. Those soundtracks became imprinted for a lifetime in my brain and heart. I gained a great appreciation for that music and loved the fact my father had performed many of those tunes on many occasions. His top ten Broadway plays: *Camelot, Phantom of the Opera, Carousel, The King and I, Oklahoma, South Pacific, West Side Story, Candide, The Fantasticks,* and *Les Misérables.*

One of Dad's more endearing qualities would show itself randomly. He might be in a conversation before suddenly breaking into song. For example, when he would advise me and my friends about women, which he did often, he would start belting out the lyrics to "I'm an Ordinary Man" from *My Fair Lady.* This type of behavior certainly brought a contrast to his aura as a stern disciplinarian. Those Catholic nuns would have laughed at even the suggestion of Dad being a disciplinarian given his behavior as a youth.

I think his approach came from being a perfectionist and having a drive to become better in everything he did. Do everything 100 percent and complete a task the right way. He pounded that approach into us, I think, because of an awareness about how much discourse he had created for his mother. Never would he let his kids behave the way he had. He operated more in a mode of "Do as I say, not as I did!"

Dad delivered reminders that he indeed was the family's disciplinarian, and he wasn't hesitant to deliver suggestions about how things might go if I chose to go astray. For example, sometimes he'd give me a horse bite (which is pinching, using all four fingers and thumb) really hard on my hamstring before saying, "That's for nothing. Wait until you do something." Other times, he would walk by me and hit me in the arm, offering the same comment. And believe me, that worked. I thought twice before I stepped out of line!

Even though he was a disciplinarian, I never doubted his love for me. Some things weren't expressed back then. You just knew it.

CHAPTER 5

Nicklaus and White Fang Come to Be

DAD WASN'T MUCH OF AN athlete, though he loved golf, so I'm sure he watched the 1967 U.S. Open at Baltusrol Golf Club in Springfield, New Jersey.

Jack Nicklaus had gone to Baltusrol feeling lost. He'd struggled during the first half of the 1967 golf season.

Part of the blame could be directed to his decision to start moving the ball from right to left—a draw, rather than his familiar left-to-right power fade.

Yes, he'd won the Crosby tournament at Pebble Beach early on, but the "Golden Bear" didn't have much to show for the rest of the season. Particularly frustrating was not making the cut at Augusta National, the first time in his professional career that he had not advanced to the weekend play at The Masters.

Heading into the second major of the season—the U.S. Open at Baltusrol—Jack had won just $31,321. Arnold Palmer had almost tripled him by making $91,213 to that point.

Public sentiment allowed that Jack held the status as the top golfer in the world. Another sentiment said they clearly favored Palmer with their adoration, which became apparent during the

1962 U.S. Open at Oakmont, when Jack won his first and only U.S. Open (to that point) in a playoff against Palmer. By 1967, "Arnie's Army" still represented a large contingent even though Palmer's last major title had been a win at the 1964 Masters.

Palmer limped into Baltusrol favoring a muscle spasm in his hip. And he'd given up cigarettes again after experiencing dizziness and shortness of breath during the 1967 Masters.

Though Jack had begun to find his swing by going back to the power fade, he had not putted well in 1967. *You drive for show, you putt for dough.* If he wanted to have any chance of winning the U.S. Open, he knew he had to sink some putts.

Earlier in his career, Jack had been told his putter wasn't heavy enough, so he had made a change while at the 1962 Phoenix Open, going from a Ben Sayers blade putter to a George Low Sportsman Wizard 600 model. That George Low would be in Jack's hands when he won fifteen majors and seventy-eight titles around the world.

But the George Low putter simply wasn't working for him during that period in 1967, prompting him to pack plenty of putters prior to leaving for Baltusrol the week before the tournament to play a practice round. Along with that extra baggage came the hope that he could sort from that collection a putter that felt right—a flat stick that became a magical wand in his hands, empowering him to drain putts from anywhere. Having such a feeling would not only help his putting, it would help his entire game. When a player didn't putt well, he pressed to hit the ball closer to the hole, so he could have a chance of sinking the putt. Putting well brought a carefree feeling of knowing that just hitting the ball onto the green would give him a shot at making a birdie. Jack understood having that feeling, because he'd felt that way plenty of times in the past.

Jack found himself on the putting green following a practice round. Fellow professional Deane Beman, a longtime friend and

later the PGA Tour commissioner, putted alongside him and introduced him to a Bull's Eye putter. Jack began to sink putts, creating
a connection. Something about the putter just felt right in Jack's
hands.

Beman did not give Jack that putter, but he hooked him up with
Fred Mueller, a friend of his to whom he'd given one of the putters. Mueller let Jack use it. The only difference between the putter
Beman used and the one he'd given to Mueller was the color of the
head, which Mueller had painted white to reduce glare.

After making the equipment change, Jack shot an 8-under-par
62 the following week in his final practice round at Baltusrol. At
the time, he'd never shot a lower round in the United States, though
he'd once shot a 62 in Australia.

The good news for Jack came in the satisfaction of shooting 62.
The bad news came in the fretting that followed. Had he wasted his
best effort during a practice round?

Baltusrol first hosted the U.S. Open in 1903. Willie Anderson
won the championship that year with a 308 on the Old Course.
Baltusrol's Old Course hosted one more U.S. Open, and the Upper
Course hosted one. The Lower Course first hosted a U.S. Open
in 1954, then again in 1967, which proved to be the fifth time
the historic site hosted the tournament recognized as the national
championship.

IBM introduced a computer-generated scoreboard at this U.S.
Open, allowing the gallery to better follow the action through
instant updates, rather than having to be dependent on results via
hand-delivered messages.

On the first day of the tournament, amateur Marty Fleckman,
a three-time All-American at the University of Houston, shot a
3-under-par 67. A thunderstorm then interrupted play, preventing
fifteen players in the field of 150 from finishing the opening round.
Golfers have long joked about pulling out a 2-iron when lightning

begins to strike, because not even God can hit a 2-iron. In reality, players aren't that cavalier. They headed for the clubhouse at the first hint of lightning.

Jack completed his round before the interruption, posting a 71, a score many would love to have in a U.S. Open. Yet relative to the 62 he'd shot in the previous day's practice round, 71 felt disappointing. He'd made just one birdie and needed thirty-five putts to complete his round. Jack's 62 saw him make eight birdies and use just twenty-eight putts.

Sweltering temperatures for the second round prompted the placement of cold water at each tee. Palmer noted: "I didn't want to start drinking too much, because I knew that once I started, I'd never stop."

Obviously, they didn't know much about hydration at the time.

Ben Hogan said that even Texas weather felt cooler than what they were experiencing at Baltusrol, prompting the surly golf legend to comment: "Hot? Hell can't be any hotter. I'll check that out one of these days."

Despite the heat, a record second-day crowd of 20,819 showed. Thirty would be treated for heat exhaustion by the Red Cross. Those who remained standing saw Fleckman shoot 73 and fall to fourth place, while Jack recovered to shoot 67, placing him second.

Afterward, Jack told reporters that he'd weighed 207 pounds when he teed off. By his estimate, he'd sweated off seven pounds after eighteen holes, leaving him at about 200 pounds. Guzzling sweet tea proved to be the perfect tonic for helping his recovery from being out in the heat.

Putting led the way for Jack's four-shot improvement in the second round. Critical among those putts was the ten-footer he'd sunk on the par-3 No. 4. If Jack had missed that putt, he would have been two over for the day and three over for the tournament.

Jack managed two birdies on the front to card a 33, followed by three birdies on the back side. Feeling at home with his new putter, Jack had needed just thirty-one putts to navigate Baltusrol's treacherous greens.

Palmer led the tournament, and he'd needed just sixty-three putts in two rounds. Both Jack and Palmer were striking the ball well and probably would have gone crazy low had Baltusrol's greens not brought such a mind game to the field. Still, neither Jack nor Palmer had three-putted during the first two rounds.

Palmer had never led the U.S. Open after two rounds.

Heading into the third round, defending champion Billy Casper trailed by one shot. The 1966 U.S. Open had been held at the Lake Course of the Olympic Club in San Francisco and witnessed Casper's miraculous comeback that saw him fight back to tie Palmer, who had led him by seven strokes heading into the back nine on Sunday. That forced an eighteen-hole playoff the following day, which Casper won.

Jack and Palmer were paired together for the third round. They had not been paired in a group during a major tournament since the 1962 U.S. Open at Oakmont. Jack vs. Arnie had an odd effect on the heavyweights. Both seemed to compete as if involved in match play rather than competing against the scoreboard. In short, being matched against each other affected both adversely.

According to *Sports Illustrated*, Jack recognized the effect they were having on each other and told Palmer on the eighth tee: "Let's stop playing each other and play the golf course."

Jack finished the third round with a 72, which meant he would head to the final round tied with Casper and Palmer for second. Fleckman had rallied to lead the tournament by a shot.

The heat had continued to scorch Baltusrol during the third round, though 92 degrees registered four degrees under the high from the second round. Still, the Red Cross continued to be busy, treating twenty-five spectators for heat exhaustion. Taking a proactive approach, they handed out 1,500 salt tablets during the third round as compared to four hundred the previous day.

Because, like today, the United States Golf Association's system made its pairings based on the order of scoring, Fleckman and Casper were paired up for the final round. Fleckman stood at 209, and Casper had been the first to post 210, leaving Jack and Palmer—also at 210—to once again be paired up for Sunday's round.

That's when Jack got busy, getting locked in from the start. Using the putter that acquired the nickname "White Fang," Jack sank a twelve-foot birdie putt on the third hole, a four-footer for birdie on the fourth hole, and a thirteen-foot birdie on No. 5. After making bogey on No. 6, Jack sank birdie putts of twenty-two and twelve feet on the seventh and eighth holes, respectively. Jack three-putted the tenth hole, then played the remaining eight holes without a bogey while sinking birdie putts of four feet on No. 13 and five feet on No. 14. On No. 18, Nicklaus found trouble after hitting his tee ball into the rough, which he followed with a fat lay-up shot using an 8-iron. That left him 230 yards from the pin. But a well-struck 1-iron eased any anxiety by leaving him twenty-two feet from the pin. With White Fang in hand, he sank the putt for birdie to finish with a 65, good for a U.S. Open record-setting five-under 275. Hogan had held the record since 1948 when he fired 276 at the Riviera Country Club in Los Angeles.

Palmer shot 69 to finish four shots behind Jack. Casper came in at 72, while Fleckman blew up, shooting 80, which meant he would not become the first amateur to win the U.S. Open since Johnny Goodman in 1933.

Jack won four additional PGA Tour titles using the Bull's Eye before the putts quit dropping, prompting him to change putters and retire White Fang.

CHAPTER 6

Exposure to Golf and on to Team Sports

As DAD STARTED WORKING AND raising a family, he joined The Country Club of Miami. Golf immortal Bobby Jones was the architect for the complex that had two 18-hole courses—East and West—along with a par-3 course that no longer exists.

The National Airlines Open used to be held there. Attending those tournaments with Dad, I got to see the likes of Jack Nicklaus, Lee Trevino, and Gay Brewer play. That helped fan the flames for my interest in the sport.

The clubhouse sat on a big hill with a grandiose entrance, at least it was to an eight-year-old in 1970. Moving to the back, the club had a cafeteria and a huge bar—remember that's back when the two-martini lunch and happy hour were all part of day-to-day life. That bar overlooked a practice putting green, which sat between the East and the West courses. Among the many lakes and creeks on the course, there was a small creek that ran alongside the eighteenth green on the East course. I refined my talent for catching fish at that creek using bread balls on a hand line to reel in bream, blue gill, and bass. Fishing got easier when I got my first Zebco the next Christmas.

The house of Jackie Gleason (known as "Ralph Cramden" on "The Honeymooners") stood next to the eighteenth hole of the West Course. The "Great One" represented Miami Beach, and his u-shaped, single-story house ranked as one of the largest built on the course. I'd never seen a bigger house at the time. Ranch-style had been popular with most of the old Florida homes. People didn't think having to supply air conditioning for two floors would be practical, because hot air rose. Other weird theories existed about why a single-story house worked better in Florida than a two-story.

I'd see Gleason out on the course from time to time, or in his backyard. Later, Dad took me to one of his shows, which were filmed at the Miami Beach Auditorium. Gleason's final variety series featured sketches from "The Honeymooners," along with marquee guest stars—an Ed Sullivan-type show. I didn't really get Jackie Gleason back then. Now his humor kills me.

It was in this environment that Dad introduced me to golf. Knowing that Dad loved golf motivated me to play the sport and try to improve. In retrospect, I can see where it afforded him the chance to share an activity with his son and to have something in which we could compete against each other. Watching him hit balls at the driving range brought me a sense of wonder. How could anybody be so strong? When he made contact, an explosion followed. The flight of the ball would start low, then reach its peak until I could no longer see it. I'd think, *Gosh, I'd love to be able to hit the ball like that.*

Junior clubs weren't easily available. No problem. Tinkerer to the rescue! Dad took my measurements, then used a hacksaw to saw off a few of his old clubs to fit me. That labor of love produced my first set of clubs. With a driver, a pitching wedge, a seven-iron, and a putter in tow, I'd play tirelessly. Man, I loved those clubs! Playing golf made me happy. I'd hit plastic balls in the front yard or putt on the carpet in the house. Putting with Dad on the putting green was what I liked best.

One day while I was hitting a ball in the front yard, my older sister, Margie, tried to steal the ball. I hurried my swing and . . . yep, you guessed it! I don't know where the ball went, but she came away with eight stitches. Thank goodness the blow struck her forehead and not her eye or her teeth.

By the time I turned eight, I could play golf well enough to tackle the par-3 course. Dad taught me what he could. Like most people trying to help their kids learn the game, he wanted me to have a proper stance and grip, because that's what he had been taught. He also had a putting quirk that he used for many years, one that I imitated when I was young, because I thought, *That's how you're supposed to do it.* While preparing to putt, he would position the putter head in front of the ball, then move the head behind the ball—something he might do several times before finally putting. I'm pretty sure he copied Jack Nicklaus.

Ultimately, Dad had the wisdom to understand he wasn't the right person to teach his son how to play golf. Babe Hart, the club's professional, assumed that role.

Hart had spent a little time on the PGA Tour. He looked as though he'd played football, standing tree-like, a big, solid oak. When he hit the ball, it disappeared like Dad's drives, only farther. Babe Hart amazed me.

The driving range sat across the street from the East Course. Hart used to land his single-engine Cessna right there on the driving range, and you could see it from the eighteenth tee.

Tournaments were held at the club every summer, including the "Skipper Chuck" tournament.

"The Skipper Chuck Show" aired weekday mornings in South Florida. Chuck Zink served as the producer and announcer for the children's TV show. Zink also played "Skipper Chuck," the show's main character. The show had an unprecedented twenty-two-year run, so Zink became a local celebrity. He certainly ranked as a bigger deal to me than Jackie Gleason. Later, I found out that Zink had been progressive where desegregation was concerned. He lost the show's major sponsor, Royal Castle, because he'd refused to segregate on the show. Ironically, a fledgling company known as Burger King took over the spot and soared.

The Skipper Chuck par-3 tournaments operated like First Tee does today, affording kids an opportunity to grow their interest in golf.

While participating in one of those Skipper Chuck tournaments, I played a hole that required me to carry a lake to reach a pin set approximately 140 yards away—a daunting task for an eight-year-old. I made solid contact, cleared the lake, and landed the ball on the green. The ball hit the pin. I thought I'd made a hole in one! That further sparked my interest for the game.

When you're a kid, the prospect of driving a golf cart brought more excitement than swinging the club. One time, I rode along with Dad, and he let me move the cart. Man, I felt like big stuff. I'd been instructed to move the cart from alongside the green that he and his foursome were playing to the next tee box. That brief trip didn't go well. I turned the cart against an embankment, and the cart began to tip. I'd never seen that group of men move so fast. Fortunately, they caught the cart before it could flip. That scared me to death.

Neither golf nor tennis came easily. Initially, I didn't see a lot of success in either sport. That's probably why I eventually gravitated to team sports and left behind golf before again picking up the sport years later.

Being "The Music Man" made Dad the creative one in our family. Yet he loved every sport, just not basketball. Ironically, my mother excelled in basketball, and she loved the sport he gruffly referred to as "roundball."

Thankfully, Dad never took issue with "The Music Man's" son becoming a jock. I played baseball, basketball, and football around the clock.

He'd pushed Margie into music and had been adamant in directing her to learn to play the piano. Then he browbeat her with his heavy-handedness, stressing the importance of the classics, the scales, and other things. They would have knock-down, drag-out fights about her practicing, or lack thereof.

When I'd see the piano teacher come to the house to teach my sister, I knew sparks could fly at any minute. His name was Hollis Walsh, and he fit the mold for the stereotypical piano teacher. Round-rim glasses. Semibald. A thin mustache. A detached master, much like my father. I didn't want any part of that. Thank goodness Dad didn't push me in that direction. Yet as an adult, it is one of my great wishes that I could sit down and play the piano like my Grandma Wessel.

Why did Dad jam music down Margie's throat and not mine? I don't know, he never said. It could have been a gender thing, or perhaps the fact that she had started the lessons, and he believed that if you started something, you had to finish what you started. You do a job, you take care of the details, and you pick up after yourself. In deference to that thinking, I wanted to play the guitar, and I took a few lessons before I got frustrated and quit. Dad never said a word about me quitting. I can still play a few chords. Every now and then, I'll grab the guitar and play a little bit. But I never read music. The only thing I've kept is the love of Broadway and singing, and being around Broadway shows and Broadway tunes. Knowing my dad like I did, I think he chose not to force music on me, because he'd seen how the pursuit went with my sister. No doubt he made the right call, as active as I was with sports.

Later, after I had my own kids, I'd tease Dad that I understood what he'd been trying to accomplish. I acknowledged the frustration your children can cause you. Such as when they leave something out and walk right by it instead of putting it away. Those types of things.

Dad wasn't an absentee father, yet he missed a lot of my games. My mother rarely missed any of them. If Dad wasn't singing on the weekend, he might try to be at my game, but he didn't get the same fulfillment that my mom did from watching my sisters and me play. That just wasn't ingrained in him. Still, it meant the world to me whenever he did show. If I hit a home run, or my team won, he'd give me a wink or nod his head. Those simple gestures were all I needed. It didn't have to be words.

We became friends with the kids of my parents' friends. We spent a lot of time at the pool at the Country Club of Miami. That's where I first was introduced to diving off the board. The club had a high dive. You don't see those at country clubs anymore. Nobody had insurance concerns back then, and we didn't live in such a litigious society.

There were three diving boards—a 3-meter springboard, and two lower boards alongside it. I'd try and do one-and-a-halves and backflips. Twice I hit my head on the board and got stitches. I dislocated my thumb doing a one-and-a-half reverse dive in competition. You had to be fearless to be a diver.

That experience at the Country Club of Miami led to a lifelong appreciation for diving.

When we later moved to North Miami, I became a diver in the eighth and ninth grades at the YMCA next to our house. I dived competitively for two years.

My parents had lived in a new subdivision in Carol City when I was born. Now called Miami Gardens, it's the northern end of Dade County, located four to five miles from where the Miami Dolphins trained in their early years and where I attended high school.

The houses in our neighborhood were similar—all were single-floor and small, but they were different enough not to be classified as track housing. Our three-bedroom house had a hallway, a

Florida room, a kitchen, a carport, jalousie windows, and no central air. We had a wall unit in the Florida room and a unit in Mom and Dad's bedroom. Eventually, we all got wall units. The yard had orange and grapefruit trees and two large mango trees. Later, I took my kids to visit that house when they were ten and twelve. The first words out of their mouth were "Wow, that's dirty and awfully small." Neighborhoods and perspective change with time.

Our house stood on a corner lot where four streets merged. They weren't busy streets, though. In fact, the neighborhood felt like a sports complex.

We'd play stickball and all kinds of other games we'd invent at different locales around the neighborhood. We'd use the little fence across the street from our house to aim at when we played home run ball. You'd get certain points if you hit the ball into the neighbor's backyard. Sometimes we'd play football at the Methodist school down the street or at a field about three blocks away. When the grass on the field got too long, we'd cut a big enough patch on which we could play football. Shoes were used for boundaries. Kind of like our own "Field of Dreams" minus the cornfield.

Kids lived at most every house in the neighborhood. That made for some great pickup games. We might have ten or fifteen kids depending on the day. Kids would knock on our door trying to get Margie to play. They wouldn't even ask me. Margie could play every sport well. We had some good games even though the ages could vary greatly.

While Dad had an aversion to "roundball," his disdain for the sport didn't prevent him from fixing us up with a dual goal in our driveway. He rigged it so we could turn the goal into an eight-foot-high goal or a regulation ten-foot-high goal.

When the day's end approached and dinnertime arrived, my mother would ring her black bell like the schoolteacher she was.

We had to be home in the next five or ten minutes, or we were in trouble. That's the way you communicated long before cell phones.

When I was in eighth grade in 1975, we moved to a 1 ½-acre house on Mitchell Lake in North Miami. It was a tropical paradise with a private street that was lined with coconut palm trees. The two large trees in the Japanese garden gave us kids a great swing rope and platform to jump into the water. The property had Florida oak, poinciana, mango, avocado, and frangipani trees. The previous owner of the house left behind an orchid nursery, which pleased Dad, who assumed control, diligently tending to all the different strands of orchids, along with the staghorn ferns. All this created lots of opportunities for me, my sisters, and others to help Dad take care of the grounds. Although we were involved with many activities and sports, Dad's rule was the chores had to be finished first before we embarked on our sports.

CHAPTER 7

Alcoholics Anonymous

DAD MADE A VISIT TO the doctor in 1973. I didn't completely understand the magnitude at that time. Only later would I comprehend what happened and the changes that he made afterward.

The doctor told him he had a liver disease, and he needed to stop drinking or die.

According to a lot of research, genetics can play a role in alcoholism. It's not just your environment. When you have that gene, you either suppress it or give in and become an alcoholic.

I've heard that my grandfather had been an alcoholic. He drank and smoked. That's what his generation did. Saloons served as meeting places, just like in the Westerns. Locals went there to socialize. That was a different time, of course, when kids often started drinking at thirteen, fourteen, fifteen years old. Thus, my grandfather might have contributed to that predisposition in the family chain.

After receiving the doctor's diagnosis, Dad tried to stop drinking on his own. He couldn't do it. Finally, in 1975, he started going to Alcoholics Anonymous. He embraced wholeheartedly what the organization fed him. To my knowledge, he never touched alcohol after that and even became a staunch AA leader in South Florida for thirty-five years. Helping others became an admirable by-product of

Dad joining the AA family, but he wouldn't just give help to people without some action on their part. He felt strongly about that.

Dad held firm to the belief that you should try to help people out of hardships and assist them in transitioning into society. In other words, try and lead them toward becoming self-reliant so they can help themselves. Helping people without action on their part, to where they became reliant on the handout, crippled them in Dad's eyes. He lived his adult life trying to help those people he encountered who were less fortunate and needed that hand up, not out.

We had so many people come to the house who were complete strangers. Dad would bring them over to help in the yard or to help with any number of tasks, such as assisting in our addition to the house.

Dad's work projects weren't exclusive to wayward souls from AA, either. If you spent the night at our house, you were fair game to become part of a work party.

On one occasion during my freshman year of high school in the fall of 1975, Jimmy Metz came over and spent the night at my house. The following day brought dark skies and light showers. That didn't stop Dad, who got us out of bed and put us to work trimming an oak tree that was leaning over the lake. All day long, we chopped and carried limbs out to the front. After that, Jimmy went to school and told everybody, "Mr. Wessel's crazy, you don't want to spend the night over there. He just wants to put you to work!"

Jimmy never stayed over again. I couldn't blame him.

Because I had been younger when Dad got sober, I wasn't as tuned into how sobriety affected him, until, as an adult, I started to reflect on that time. It was then that I began to realize that when Dad drank, he'd been emotional, quick-tempered, and had mood swings. I never saw him be abusive, but I do believe there were difficulties, arguments, and fights that probably would not have taken place had he not been drinking.

Avoiding the alcohol journey would have taken an exceptional effort on his part given his circumstances, like hanging with older guys when he entered the Navy at fifteen. Chasing women and drinking alcohol, no doubt, had to be a priority for the sailors who were on the ship with him.

What I always found admirable, though, was his discipline and courage. The serenity prayer that was adopted by AA and other twelve-step programs became Dad's mantra for how he lived his life—with acceptance of that for which he had no control and bravery to work on what he could change, along with constant prayer to have the wisdom to distinguish between the two. I am sure it was especially difficult on golf trips or just a weekend round with his golfing buddies. His 19th hole didn't include his having an alcoholic beverage. I'm so proud of my father's discipline and courage over the years facing this disease, even when around others who drank.

CHAPTER 8

Hanging with the Miami Dolphins

My parents were adamant about being polite and engaging with others. They believed that you never knew when someone would come into your life. When that happens, connections are created that can change or create other connections that can/will influence your life. For me and my life, Dorothy Shula, the wife of Hall of Fame football coach Don Shula, became the connection that opened the door for me. Not only did she enable me to experience up close and personal the Miami Dolphins of the 1970s and the 1980s, but so much of my life, including my entrée to football, I can trace back to her connection to my mother.

Hialeah Miami Lakes High School opened its doors in 1971. Mom worked there as the assistant principal for guidance. The Wessel family's personal connection to the Dolphins began the day Dorothy Shula walked into Mom's office.

Dorothy asked Mom for her opinion: would she send her kids to Miami Lakes? Mom told her she would send them to the Catholic High School, Pace High.

The Shulas ended up sending their first son, David, to Pace High. And through that first meeting, Mom and Dorothy began to play cards together, forming a relationship that lasted until Dorothy died of cancer in 1991.

Thus, Mom's ability to engage with people and make them feel welcome laid the groundwork for my future in football as a player and a coach.

Don Shula played for the Cleveland Browns, Baltimore Colts, and Washington Redskins. He became head coach of the Colts, then moved on to the Miami Dolphins, where he coached the 17–0 team in 1972.

As for Dad, he had been a Dolphins season-ticket holder from the beginning, when they were an expansion team in the old AFL. I started to attend games with him during the 1970 season, when I was eight.

Going to those games would be quite an affair. Our drive to the Orange Bowl would take us about thirty minutes. Dad and his friends packed their trunks with coolers filled with food and beverages so we could tailgate. The adults would sit around shooting the bull before the game while the kids threw around the football on a grass parking lot outside the Orange Bowl end zone.

Once inside the historic venue, I enjoyed many memorable Dolphins moments sitting next to Dad.

Dad went to New Orleans when the Dolphins made their first Super Bowl appearance in 1972. They got smoked, 24–3, by the Dallas Cowboys at Tulane Stadium.

When they won the Super Bowl the next season, they beat the Redskins 14–7 at the Los Angeles Coliseum on January 14, 1973. That proved to be a big day in my neighborhood. Everybody went out into the street to celebrate the win.

Along with Shula, Howard Schnellenberger joined the Dolphins' coaching staff in 1970. His wife, Beverlee, also asked Mom for advice about schools. She joined the card group, which included Betty Jane Arnsparger, wife of Dolphins coach Bill Arnsparger. Through my mother's connection, I met one of the Schnellenbergers' sons, Stu, in 1975, and we became friends, teammates on the high school football team, and workout partners.

Mom's friendship with Beverlee and Dorothy grew. As a Dolphins fan, Dad enjoyed that connection, as well.

Meanwhile, Mom's friendship with them, and my friendship with Stu, opened the door for me to know Shula's sons. Those relationships also bought me entry to the Dolphins' training camp at Biscayne College (now known as St. Thomas University) in the summer before my junior year at Pace High School, which sat on the same plot of land as the college.

Stu and I worked for janitorial services at Biscayne. We picked up jocks, took out trash, that sort of stuff. Our menial jobs didn't mean much to us. What mattered were the afternoons when we'd get to work out with the Dolphins. That proved to be my first exposure to the NFL. That taste of the NFL made a lasting impression on a fifteen-year-old.

Talk about a kid's dream. What I experienced was a fantasy. I found myself getting to know the guys who comprised the team I'd watched and admired. When I'd played neighborhood football games, I'd pretended to be any one of the Dolphins players. They were the guys who had done all that winning. Shula's first eight seasons coaching in Miami saw the Dolphins going 83–28. I'm sure Dad was just as excited as I was about my chance to be around them, though he low-keyed that kind of stuff. He'd been around celebrities, so he wasn't particularly impressed by fame.

Since we lived in Carol City, we were four to five miles north of Biscayne College. Miami Lakes was about ten miles away. That's where Shula and Schnellenberger lived.

Mom and Dad would occasionally get invited to parties over at their houses.

Some of the players from the Dolphins' undefeated season were still on the team when I first started hanging around them. Some were on the tail end of their careers. Did they ever talk about their undefeated season? Oh God yes. There were always references back to that 17–0 season, which seemed to have had a life of its own.

Bob Kuechenberg served as the ringleader for a weekly Friday ritual during training camp. He and the other linemen shot the bull around a cooler stocked with Busch beer, which many would drink until they couldn't move. Some of them smoked cigarettes. The equipment managers, Dan Dowe and Bob Monica, were all about the linemen. They catered to Kooch, Jim Langer, Larry Little, and Norm Evans. On occasion, they would let others in their group, but everybody knew the group belonged to the offensive line.

As for Larry Csonka, I didn't know him well. In fact, he terrified me. But he was always the prankster. He's the one who put a little three-foot alligator in Coach Shula's shower. He was always doing something to get the coaches riled up.

Shula was old school. You never saw such a perfectionist. He strived for perfection in everything he did.

Schnellenberger maintained a gruff manner. You always felt as though he were sizing you up, like, "Why are you here?" Adding to his persona, he smoked a pipe and had a deep voice, which helped sculpt a scary figure. Shula and Schnellenberger weren't shy about bringing discipline to the team. The players talked about that fact all the time.

Arnsparger came from another angle as a quiet leader. In contrast, Shula was a little more vibrant. Of course, this was my perspective as a kid. At the time, I didn't have the coach's lens I would later have.

Defensive linemen Bob Baumhower and A.J. Duhe were friends and called themselves "Peanut Butter and Jelly," because Baumhower was from University of Alabama and Duhe was from LSU. Of course, Stu and I mimicked them and started calling ourselves "Peanut Butter and Jelly."

I didn't think much about how being around all of those guys affected me, as I was too wrapped up in the experience. Later I would realize that being around people who had some measure of fame helped me understand they weren't any different from me. I think that taught me a good lesson—not to be intimidated by such public figures.

Of course, the funny thing about childhood is that you never quite know where people are going to wind up. Around my junior year, I came to know Harry Wayne Casey, better known as KC, the leader of the world-renowned KC and the Sunshine Band.

Though KC reigned as a megastar in the 1970s, to us, he was just the Schnellenbergers' neighbor.

I met him my junior year of high school at a party at the Schnellenbergers' house.

The Schnellenbergers were home, so I wouldn't classify the party as a raucous high school party, but more like a hangout of sorts. After KC and I were introduced, we had a conversation about water skiing.

I'd been water skiing since I was eight, thanks to Dad and his love of the water. When we went fishing, we'd carry along the water skis and ski on our way to shore after we put away the fishing gear. Dad was a good water skier, in part because he grew up at the beach, and he had all kinds of friendships he could tap into for different water activities, including water skiing. Through Dad's relationships, I knew some people at a boat shop near our house. I told KC I'd get him a deal on a slalom ski if he wanted me to help him.

At the end of the party, about ten of us went over to KC's house, where I met some of his bandmates. It was there that KC took me up on my offer, and I got him a deal on a slalom ski. After that, we started water skiing with him on the lake where he lived.

Even though KC was at the height of his popularity, fame didn't go to his head. I always found him down-to-earth, and not some big shot with entitlement issues. He liked being around younger people—appropriate, I guess, because young people comprised his audience and were the ones buying his albums.

He was on the road a lot back then, but when he wasn't, we would water ski and hang out. He'd get us tickets to concerts in the Miami area, and yes, there were some pretty good parties we attended. Girls were never scarce, especially at his Christmas party. I was never "in the band," but hanging out with them made me feel like I was at times.

Bill Chastain spoke with KC during the writing process, and KC recalled the early days of our friendship:

"Because I loved music so, I wanted to put myself in the position where I was just happy doing anything associated with what I loved. So I tried to share my personal philosophy with Joe. He was just a very ambitious guy. He was really into sports, and he really wanted to have a career in football."

I felt close to KC, and so did my family. As KC recalled, "Joe and I spent a lot of time together. We talked a lot. I got to know his family, too. The whole family is just very caring and kind. They devoted their lives to charities, and people. And being a part of the community. You just got that kind of feeling from them. Once you met them, you felt like a part of their family."

All these years later, I appreciated KC's remarks, particularly regarding my family, who served a critical role in my formative years, though I never really considered their impact on my friends. When, ultimately, my janitorial job abruptly ended, leaving me without a job for the remainder of the summer, I feared the reaction of my parents (as most kids my age would have). Yet Dad emerged as my greatest ally. I think he remembered being young and having to work to make money. That experience had prevented him from doing some of the things that he'd wanted to do. He told me, "Joe, you're going to have the rest of your life to work. You've got football.

You keep working at your football, and I'll make sure you're taken care of from a work standpoint." As usual, Dad was spot on. Not having to work eliminated one pressure in my life at that time and gave me more time to lift, work out, run, and throw to wide receivers. What a blessing afforded to me by Dad.

CHAPTER 9

High School to Prep School

So it was that dad opened the door for me to live and breathe sports. In fact, I couldn't get enough of them. I played baseball, basketball, and football when I got to Monsignor Edward Pace High School, a Catholic school in Opa-locka.

Baseball probably was my best sport, even though I didn't make the team my freshman year. I've always had an "alpha male" personality, which made playing catcher on the baseball team, quarterback on the football team, and point guard on the basketball teams perfect matches.

I'm particularly thankful that I played basketball, which allowed me to get to know John Stack, who had transferred to Pace High and would become my best friend. In addition to a big heart, John had a pretty good jump shot that later earned him a scholarship to Biscayne College.

Though we met through basketball, mostly I think John and I clicked due to of our love of music.

We enjoyed the same bands, like Styx—"Come Sail Away"—and Boston. And we were late bloomers. We talked about girls a lot. My parents loved John, and he quickly became the brother who I never had and helped me through the chaos that is high school (though my friendship with Stu didn't go away; we were still very close, because of football). Despite my prowess when it came to baseball and the social lessons gained on the basketball court, it was my experience as a football player that would come to define my athletic career. I'll never forget my junior year, when we first ran the wishbone.

I liked running that offense. I found it fun, and different. Air Force, Navy, and Georgia Tech run similar offenses today. We didn't have the same type of athletes that some of the schools we played did. That offense helped even the playing field a little bit, since there weren't a lot of teams running the offense. Defenses would have to be strict on their assignments to stop the wishbone. Some of the teams we played didn't have the discipline to stick to their assignments. That's not an easy task.

We went 3–7 my junior season. Of course, I got blown up in the middle of that season against Pompano Ely. A guy hit me on my shoulder when I went to make a pitch on the option. That hit knocked me out of the game and broke my collarbone, which kept me from playing basketball indefinitely, though I did manage to recover from the injury quickly enough to play baseball my junior season, when we won the state championship.

In the spring of 1979 prior to the start of my senior season, our head football coach, Dennis Hartnett, must have gotten some help from Howard Schnellenberger in changing our offense. We went from the wishbone to a passing attack. Talk about 180 degrees difference, as those offenses were the polar opposites of each other.

Coach Schnellenberger had been the Dolphins' offensive coordinator since the 1975 season. The 1978 season would be Howard's last with the Dolphins before he moved on to make his mark as the head coach at the University of Miami in the fall of 1979.

I never asked Howard if he got involved in our offense. I figured he met with Coach Hartnett, and he helped him formulate the pass patterns and the formations. Think about how lucky we were to have a guy who coached for a professional football team offering advice to our coach about how to run our offense!

As the quarterback, I went from reading defenses, and either keeping the ball and turning up the field or handing off to a back, like I did while running the option, to where I found myself on most plays dropping back and throwing the football.

Earl Morrall, my old friend from the days working around the Dolphins, had taught me how to better throw a football. How lucky could a kid get? Morrall had won the NFL's Most Valuable Player Award for the 1968 season after stepping in for an injured Johnny Unitas and leading the Baltimore Colts to the Super Bowl. In the Dolphins' undefeated season in 1972, Bob Griese broke his ankle in the fifth game of the year. Earl came in and led them to twelve of the seventeen straight wins. And this guy would be the guy giving me some direction and a better idea about what I was doing when I wanted to throw the ball? Wow.

Earl had a unique throwing motion. He didn't throw like most quarterbacks, who throw like baseball catchers. You wouldn't see him just put the ball into position at his shoulder and snap off a throw like a catcher trying to throw out a base stealer. Everything with him was more of an above-the-shoulder throw. Earl guided me through everything, working on my footwork, my peripheral vision, and how to read defenses. Those little tips here and there helped more than anything.

That year, thanks in part to Earl, things seemed to be shaping up for me. On the football field, the coaches had us switch to a full pro-style offense. I figured I could play my way to a football scholarship somewhere. After all, I loved playing football, and the new offense appeared to be the ticket that would make me more attractive to colleges scouting for talent. By the end of my senior season, I'd thrown for 1,500 yards and earned All-State honors.

Due to these positive results, I thought that my future would include going to college on a football scholarship. Unfortunately, what I hoped for and reality produced different outcomes.

I couldn't understand why the colleges weren't looking my way—frustrating for a kid who had dedicated so much time to the pursuit of sports, and thus the thought never occurred to me that my sports career had run its course. I couldn't, and wouldn't, acknowledge such a possibility. You could say I had a blind spot about the subject. My mind refused to go in that direction, at least initially.

Ultimately, I first recognized it after we played Belle Glade High School. They had a good team, and I had completed 10 of 12 passes for 154 yards in the first half alone. Miami and Duke coaches had been at the game. I thought they'd at least come up and talk to me afterward. I mean, I was the kid who worked out with the Dolphins. Earl Morrall had been my private quarterback coach and was now the UM QB coach. Yet the college coaches weren't interested. Nobody was. That took the wind out of my sails. I thought I'd done well and that my body of work would count for something. On top of that, schools were all over Stu trying to recruit him.

One part of me felt happy for Stu, who signed a football scholarship at Duke University. Another part of me felt jealous, even though I knew that Stu was everything college coaches wanted. Somewhere in the back of my mind, I thought I could ride the coattails of Stu's success, like colleges would want to include me in a package with him. I didn't know what I'd later know when I became a coach: I wouldn't have recruited a player like me, either.

Yet my parents made sure I never quit, even though everything suggested I should. Aside from that, though, Dad seemed to feel that I needed to wear this one myself. Though I'm not sure that I made the right decision in the short term, I'm glad that Dad had encouraged me to figure out my options.

Coach Schnellenberger just started his tenure as the head coach at Miami, so I went to him looking for some perspective on my situation. He suggested I go to either a prep school or a junior college, because I needed an extra year of preparation.

Playing football at a prep school didn't count against your college eligibility. Having no scholarship offers forced my hand, and I decided to attend prep school at Fork Union Military Academy in Fork Union, Virginia, starting in the fall of 1979, to continue pursuing my football dream.

In hindsight, I probably should have thought more about playing baseball. I had more talent as a baseball player, and my size wasn't an issue on the diamond. Football just ranked higher with me. Baseball simply wasn't as fun.

Fork Union would have some athletes from time to time. Basketball star Melvin Turpin attended Fork Union when I went there. He would become one of the University of Kentucky's "Twin Towers" along with Sam Bowie, and he later played in the NBA. Future Heisman Trophy winner and No. 1 pick of the NFL draft, Vinny Testaverde, attended Fork Union after I left. Also, Eddie George attended Fork Union before winning the Heisman at Ohio State.

Colonel Red Pulliam served as the commandant and head football coach at Fork Union. I'm telling you, Dad and Red were brothers from different mothers.

Coach Pulliam was a man of few words and led through discipline. But just like Dad offered some tough love at times, once you peeled back the hard surface of Coach Pulliam, you found a compassionate man with a big heart. He cared about his players and wanted to see them succeed. The players' success was the lifeblood of the school, but he genuinely cared for all of us.

Prep schools could schedule games against college JV teams back then.

We played against freshmen teams from Navy, North Carolina, North Carolina State, William & Mary, and Richmond.

Fork Union proved to be the perfect destination for me, giving me another year of football. Coach Schnellenberger had been spot on, as that's exactly what I needed. While I worked hard at Fork Union to play well enough to reach my goal of playing college football, I experienced one of the saddest periods of my life.

Several weeks before I was about to leave for school during the summer of 1979, I got the news that John Stack got diagnosed with a rare form of leukemia and would be heading to St. Jude's Children's Hospital in Memphis, Tennessee.

We'd trained together all that summer, lifting weights, running, getting our bodies and minds ready for our next phase of life, a phase we all take for granted. Like many other teenagers, we thought we were bulletproof—only John wasn't wearing a bulletproof vest that summer.

John went to Memphis the second or third week of August. I would have gone there with him, but I'd already left for Fork Union. His family sent me a picture of him. He wore a black Grateful Dead t-shirt with the skull and crossbones. The irony of the shirt hit me when I saw it.

Back then, the mortality rate for leukemia stood at around 98 percent, meaning only 2 percent diagnosed with leukemia lived. They didn't have the treatments then that they have now.

When John first began getting treatment, I don't think he thought he was going to die. He did know he had a grave disease, though. John fought like a warrior through the torture, pain, and devastation of his physical body. In between my football and classwork at Fork Union, I tried to visit him on two occasions. Each time I tried, he'd gotten sick and couldn't be around others. His condition made him very susceptible to other complications.

John remained positive through the first couple of months. Then he started making jokes about the girls, like, "Hey if I don't make it, make up for it." He tried to maintain a great attitude, but his condition worsened.

In a letter to my parents that fall, I wrote the following about John:

He is going to make it I know. He has too many people behind him. He needs us and we need him.

In that same letter, I updated my parents on my prospects to catch on with a college for a football scholarship, or at least the prospects of becoming a walk-on where I might have the opportunity to earn a scholarship. Here's how that pursuit was going according to the letter:

Well, I just got out of Pulliam's office. He said that William & Mary would be a good choice for me. He said Notre Dame I would have a tough time. He mentioned Lafayette. He said that Dan Henning is probably going to get the William & Mary job. Hope so. He said that no one is there to look at the film at William & Mary. He was going to send it to Georgia Tech first. He said that I can take the Virginia film at Christmas break to Tulane.

While I worried about the prospects of a football scholarship, John battled for his life. They pumped him with huge doses of chemo. They figured his big body could take it. Instead, that treatment demoralized him while whittling down his body to nothing. I set up another visit to see him, but the night before I was scheduled to leave, I received a note during study hall to report to the Commandant's office. It was there that I learned that John had died on December 7, 1979, Pearl Harbor Day. Though it's been almost forty years, I remember that night like it was yesterday.

It snowed, leaving several inches on the ground. The barracks were settling in for the night. Sitting on a bench at our parade ground, I couldn't understand how God could let this happen to somebody so good, so vibrant, so full of life, and so faithful in our shared Catholic faith. The loss hurt so badly, I felt like I couldn't breathe. I just sat there reliving all of our days of fun and what we shared over the previous three years. We had a bond that would never be broken. We often compared our bond to the 1971 movie *Brian's Song*. I never could have guessed that we would have lived out the story of Brian Piccolo.

The final words that John Stack wrote to me were as follows: "Joe, remember all the good times we had. I finally have someone who I can be myself with. I love you brother. And get that scholarship."

Of course, Dad was there for me through a truly harrowing time. Harold Kushner wrote a book in 1981 titled *When Bad Things Happen to Good People*. He dedicated the book to the memory of his young son, Aaron, who died from an incurable disease at the age of fourteen. Later Dad gave me that book while I still struggled to make sense out of the death of the brother I never had.

Prior to John's death, I never felt such pain and loss. I prayed often that I may never experience that again in my life. But that's not how life is. Life is precious, because it is fleeting. Looking back at having gone through something that painful at an early age, I'm not sure how many people have that happen to them. It did give me a sense of "I got through the first one, I can get through the next one, too."

John's family gave a viewing to a few close friends. I'll never forget how emaciated he was. He'd been a strapping 225 pounds. When he died, he weighed 160.

Dad had visited John when he had business in Memphis. He came back with a dog he found somewhere and decided to name him Memphis. We had that dog for many years, and he served as a great companion and a great reminder of John's struggles at St. Jude's.

As far as offering soothing words of comfort to his only son, my father's way back then was short and meaningful. He wasn't about to let me wallow in pity. Grieving was okay, but we have to move on.

"Life is full of sadness," he told me. He also encouraged me to take John's remembrance with me in everything I did. I embraced that thought. I can't tell you how many times working out or running that I wanted to stop or quit. Then the memory of John would kick in, and I would think he would love to have the opportunity I have. Doing what I was doing at that moment. Keep going!

Gerry Sandusky (not to be confused with the now-notorious Jerry Sandusky, formerly of Penn State), who played basketball at Cooper City High School and went on to play basketball at Towson State, was friends with me and John, as well. His father worked as the offensive line coach for the Dolphins, and their family had already seen tragedy when Gerry lost his brother, who played football at Tulsa. We would we see each other on school breaks, and we used to have deep talks about John and Gerry's brother, too, how their deaths left such an empty hole in our lives. Why did they die and not us? I think those conversations helped me navigate the grieving process to some degree. But there's another part of me that never really recovered from John's death.

Gerry ended up playing tight end on the football team his last two years at Towson.

There are few friends in life that you come across and with whom you may not talk on a daily or weekly basis. Yet when you do, you just pick up where you left off the last time you spoke with them. Gerry Sandusky is that type of friend. Our relationship has always been one of mutual admiration, and we always seemed to confide in each other. I think from day one we just connected. We had mutual interests, we saw each other for who we were, we both lost a person dear to us to tragic illness, and we both had goals in our life both on the field of play and off. He also is the best Howard Cosell impersonator you will ever hear and has maintained his sense of humor through the peaks and valleys of his life. Gerry and I speak once or twice a year still. He has been the sports director for

WBAL in Baltimore for the last 20-plus years and is the play-by-play announcer for the Baltimore Ravens.

Thanks to friends like Gerry, I was able to take Dad's advice and keep going through it all. Not that it was easy. During my only football season at Fork Union, I injured my throwing hand in the fifth game. Our defensive coordinator came over to me while I was stretching and asked if I'd ever played defense. I told him no, and he said, "You can't throw. You want to play defense?"

I wanted to be on the field, and defense looked like my only choice. Next thing I knew, I was playing defensive back, against the North Carolina freshman team.

In time, defense suited me, and I thought that might be my ticket to continue playing football, since I played it well. Only there were no scholarship offers at the end of the season. Nobody even gave me a look other than William and Mary, then they didn't want to take me, because I needed another ten points on my SAT. VMI and The Citadel were possibilities, but I didn't want to stay in the military academies. After high school, I'd counted on Duke and Miami showing some interest in me. The prospect of one, or both, wanting me had played a part in my decision to attend Fork Union. Their minimal interest motivated me, but they never called. I had no interest from any schools other than the University of Virginia, which flirted with me about the possibility of walking on. They never got back to me.

If John's death hadn't been enough, the scholarship thing, or lack thereof, began to really demoralize me, and I voiced my anger on both fronts to Dad.

In a letter dated February 28, 1980, I wrote:

Dear Dad,
I really can't wait to get home. This place is really for the birds. I have a lot of things that we have to talk about and I'm not going to even try to write about them all, I'll just wait till I get home

and we'll talk. There are a couple of things that are important now and are on my mind. First is the scholarship bullcrap. Dad, I'm getting so disgusted with the whole situation. I know you and Mom keep telling me something is going to turn up. Well, as the days go by and the weeks go by, they turn into months and still not a damn word. What really surprises me is that I haven't even been approached by the likes of schools like Randolph-Macon, VMI, Citadel. I mean everyone has at least heard something from them. But not me. I know I came up here to grow, get stronger, mature and get my SAT's up, but you know and I know the real reason why I came up here and that was to get a scholarship. I know Mom tries to look at the bright sides of things and I should, too, but it's hard to look at the bright side when the dark side is so dark.

Second of all, if you're not a blue chip, you're worthless. I'll tell you a story that really turns me off. I can't believe people can be such big liars. I was with Ronnie at North Carolina and one of the coaches asked me what I played. I told him. He said that they had their fill of DB's and QB's, and that they used up their 30 scholarships. One week later they signed a QB/DB that was no bigger than I was. Today I found out that one of our linemen that played for us signed with LSU. LSU told me four weeks ago that they used up all their scholarships. LSU contacted the kid three weeks after I got the letter from them. You know what else surprises me is that I haven't heard a word from Richmond, and William & Mary. I thought for sure I should of heard from them. At least an interest letter. Dad, I've really been thinking about my future. I say to myself one-hundred times a day, "Maybe you're just not good enough." Maybe I'm not but I just can't end like this. I'll have a sour taste in my mouth for as long as I live. Tell me what you think about this? . . .

Dad responded with his direct approach that I should stay the course, and that good things were destined to come my way.

Despite the disappointment of not having any football offers, and the uncertainty about my future, I continued to participate in athletics at Fork Union. I competed in diving. I ran indoor track. And I played baseball, which allowed me to get to know the volunteer baseball coach, Jackie Jensen. Initially, I had no clue who he was.

Turns out Jackie had played in the major leagues from 1950 to 1961, and he'd earned American League Most Valuable Player honors in 1958 while playing for the Boston Red Sox. He hit thirty-five home runs during that MVP season, and he led the league with 122 runs batted in. Jackie would have played longer, but he retired in his early thirties due to an intense fear of flying.

In college, Jackie played for the University of California and became the first to play in the Rose Bowl, the World Series, and the baseball All-Star Game.

He'd been an All-American running back in 1948, his junior season at Cal, becoming the school's first player to rush for 1,000 yards in a season. Jackie placed fourth in the Heisman Trophy voting the year Doak Walker won the award.

Jackie was such a genuine individual. He would drive the vans with us to games. I'd sit up front, and we'd talk about baseball. His first wife had been his high school girlfriend, Zoe Ann Olsen, who won the silver medal in diving at the 1948 Summer Olympics. Since I competed in diving, that triggered a couple of conversations. Jackie had a soft-spoken way. What he said about the baseball swing made sense. Of course, you bought in given the weight of his background. He had a pretty impressive backside of his baseball card. Jackie encouraged me to switch-hit, and I started hitting home runs from both sides of the plate, which I'd never done before. I played well enough to garner three or four offers from small colleges in Virginia to play baseball. Of course, baseball offers are never worth much. They only cover a portion of the tuition.

I learned a great lesson from Jackie that I employ every day in my business life. He didn't try to change my swing; rather, he took the ability I had and continued to give me tips. Then he let me decide the course of direction. Similarly, throughout my business career, I have hired different people who bring their unique talents with them every day. My job is to help them develop those talents, give them tips or thoughts on how to succeed, give them empowerment, and then get out of the way so they can do what they do.

Jackie Jensen certainly enriched my baseball experience at Fork Union.

He taught me so much about baseball and a lot of other things. I stayed in touch with him for a little bit after Fork Union, prior to his sudden death in 1982.

Despite being surrounded by great mentors like Jackie, I was still in search of an opportunity to play college football. During Fork Union's spring break, my Dad and I took my sister Margie back to FSU, where she starred in volleyball. During that visit, I managed to arrange a visit with Bobby Bowden. A family friend, Bill Dawkins, who had been an All-American linebacker at FSU, had already put in a call for me. Dawkins and my mom were classmates at FSU, and he was the head coach at Miami Norland Senior High School, where my mother was the assistant principal.

When Dad and I visited Coach Bowden, we sat across from him, both of us seemingly awestruck. Coach Bowden immediately asked me in his big Southern drawl, "Were you number eighteen in that film versus North Carolina?" I told him I was. At that minute, the sale was over. I was bought and delivered.

Coach explained that he had five questions when evaluating recruits:

1. Can he graduate from FSU?
2. Is he dependable?

3. Can he run?
4. Will he fight and not quit?
5. Can we beat the Gators with him?

At the time, FSU and Nebraska were doing a lot to strengthen their programs by building up their walk-ons with "culture people." Several walk-ons had done well at FSU—Monk Bonasorte, the starting free safety, being one of them. All I wanted was a chance. So, like my mother and sister, I elected to become a Nole.

You could say Dad was pleased with the situation. For him, it was a win-win, especially with Margie already being there. Little did either of us know that it was the prospect of being a walk-on for the FSU football team and the ensuing decision to take the plunge that would one day lead to the most memorable of days that Dad and I had ever experienced together.

CHAPTER 10

FSU Early Years and the Golden Bear's Son

Prior to arriving at FSU, I spent the summer working out in Miami with the Dolphins. I continued to build my relationships with certain players there, some of whom I got to know better than others, like Earnie Rhone and Tim Foley.

Earnie taught me the sacrifice required to overcome injuries and how to remain focused when doubt crept in as a professional or even a dedicated college athlete. Man, that guy worked hard, but he remained low-key and was a man of faith—just a salt-of-the-earth kind of guy.

Tim took me under his wing and taught me how to backpedal and how to be a defensive back. Everybody looked up to Tim, who was truly a born leader and had such an influence on my life—not only in football, but also by his spiritual walk following the Christian faith. Tim openly expressed his thoughts on leadership. One of them I embraced right away, and the thought still resonates with me today. He told me if he could get the other ten players to perform at a higher level, his job would be easier. This leadership thought I carried into business and still adhere to today.

The anticipation of my freshman year had filled me with mixed emotions. I'd waited all summer to be informed about the schedule and my reporting date, but such a date never arrived. I finally decided to call George Henshaw, FSU's offensive coordinator, whom I knew, since he also performed the bulk of the recruiting in the Miami area. Coach Henshaw told me that I was not on the two-a-day reporting list. My heart sank. Disappointed, I told him Coach Bowden had told me otherwise. Coach Henshaw was about to leave on an overseas vacation, but he said he'd look into the matter before he left. I received a call the next week. They told me they got me into training camp. I can honestly say that if not for Coach Henshaw, I probably would have never played at Florida State. Frankly, I'm not sure I would have even gone to the school, as I might have tried one of the smaller Virginia schools. To say I'm eternally grateful to Coach Henshaw would be a huge understatement. When I arrived in Tallahassee that fall, I got to observe Coach Bowden. Everybody felt his charisma.

Since I played defense, I didn't see him during practices as often as the offense did. He handled things just as the CEO of a big company might handle them. Offense was his baby, so he would be hands-on where the offense was concerned, though he still let the coaches coach. But he rarely got involved with the defense. Still, he watched everything, even when you'd least expect it. He always walked around with a pencil and an oversized index card, taking notes that he would review. If he had concerns about something he wrote on that note card, he'd address that concern with the coaches and/or the team.

In the fall of 1980, Florida State football had ten All-Americans returning to the team, including Ron Simmons and Bobby Butler. They'd gone 11–0 the previous season prior to suffering a 24–7 loss to Oklahoma in the Orange Bowl. Not only did that loss dash their hopes for an undefeated season, it also cost them a shot at winning the national championship.

The 1980 team returned ten of eleven starters on defense. The loss to Oklahoma remained fresh in the coaches' minds, and they made sure that loss remained fresh in the players' minds, as well. Training camp was the most brutal I ever experienced in eighteen years of football, as a player or coach.

At the beginning of camp, a heat wave hit Tallahassee that propelled the mercury levels on the local bank's digital thermometer to 103 on consecutive days. Unlike in today's environment, freshmen arrived back then knowing that the odds of anyone getting any playing time were nil to none. As a nonscholarship walk-on who had to fight his way to get into training camp, my odds were even worse. I tried to make the best of the situation, but the never-quit attitude ingrained in me from Dad got tested daily. After the first three days with two practices per day, we put on the pads.

In the locker room, there was a list of three to four names assigned to wear this big puffy suit over your football gear during a given practice. Basically, the suit ran from your hips to your knees. Ostensibly, that new gadget helped defensive players learn how to tackle better without hurting the ball carrier. However, the suit restricted your ability to run, so the runner had difficulty running while wearing the suit.

Just picture yourself being a freshman football player and ten starters returning from one of the best defenses ever to play at FSU were running full speed at you while the coaches yelled, "Knock the snot out of him! Knock him back!"

If you cringed or shied away, the coaches made you go again. I think wearing that suit served two purposes. First, it helped the defense get better at tackling. And second, it gave the coaches insight about the players who were tough and wouldn't quit even though they had to wear the suit.

Wearing that suit brought a lot of humiliation, too. Much of the humiliation had to do with the fact that the coaches had selected you to wear the thing in the first place. But wearing the suit was like your rite of passage. Many of the older defensive players took care of the players who didn't take the easy way out. They understood how difficult being in our position could be and usually took care of you if you didn't try to embarrass them. I'm not sure if I felt more like the Michelin Man or the Pillsbury Doughboy while wearing that suit.

The varsity went 10–1 my freshman season, and I played on the junior varsity. Back then, the JV would play a five- or six-game schedule. Our main function was on the scout team, helping the varsity prepare for their next opponent. Junior varsity teams no longer exist.

Miami accounted for the only blemish on the varsity schedule that season, handing out a 10–9 loss in the Orange Bowl. Of course, good alum that he was, Dad came to mind. Because Margie and I both went to FSU, you would think he would root and pull for FSU. I would bet that if either of us were playing he would root for FSU, but if we weren't playing, he probably stayed true to the U. That's just the kind of loyalty he's always showed.

At the end of that 1980 season, FSU again headed to the Orange Bowl to play Oklahoma for a second straight year. This time, the game proved to be a close one that went down to the wire. We were winning, 17–10, with 3:19 left in the game. The FSU band already began to play the first stanza of Queen's "Another One Bites the Dust." That's when their quarterback, J.C. Watts, took the game into his hands, driving the Sooners down the field until he connected with Steve Rhodes on a touchdown pass with 1:33 remaining. Oklahoma decided to go for the win, and Watts threw a pass to Forrest Valora in the end zone for the two-point conversion that gave them a lead. Bill Capece's 62-yard field goal attempt at the end didn't have enough on it, and we lost, 18–17. That killed our chances of becoming national champions. Although I didn't play that year in any varsity games, I did dress for a couple games and the Orange Bowl, too.

Added to the daily grind was the constant reminder that I wasn't on scholarship at FSU, though I very much wanted to be, so I put a lot of pressure on myself. As had become customary, I wrote to Dad when the level of frustration had reached its peak, in a letter dated April 23, 1981:

> . . . *The pressure is starting to build up inside of me. The few mistakes I make on the field seem so giant to me because I demand perfection on my part. I feel if I'm going to make it, I have to do everything right. I'm trying to be tough in my tackling, but I must not get used to going and beating my brains out. Coach Stanton yesterday called me out to the field during the scrimmage and told me when I run the ball in drills to take on hits and work on my toughness. He said I have all the tools to make it, but I have to hit and that might hold me back. Dad, I just want to know if they are going to put me on scholarship or not. That sense of security means so much to me. At times I feel like there is no doubt they'll put me on. Then other times, I'm not so sure. Last night I sat and pondered about it and before I knew it an hour and a half passed by. I think of it constantly and I know I shouldn't. I pray every night and leave it up to God. I know he'll watch over me, I just hope what I want is what he wants . . .*

> *All my love, Joe*

> *P.S. Persistence, tenacity, and perseverance are qualities that I can only attain by a wonderful father who teaches them to me. Thanks.*

Dad and Mom both remained supportive of my efforts, and I kept after my goal of earning a scholarship and playing football for the Seminoles.

Nevertheless, there were still quite a few challenges to face. The 1981 season marked probably the hardest schedule ever put together in the modern era of college football. The schedule saw the Seminoles go to Nebraska, Ohio State, Notre Dame, Pittsburgh, and LSU in consecutive games. The press dubbed the schedule "Oktoberfest!" We also played the Gators in Gainesville the last week of the season.

I think Coach Bowden thought our athletic director had been drunk at Octoberfest when he scheduled those games. While taking on those giants sounded like suicide for any team, the strategy turned out to be brilliant. If you won those games, you had instant credibility, and your program suddenly became relevant.

The guy who influenced me the most back then—and still does today—is Brian McCrary. Brian hailed from Germantown, Tennessee, and had been a Golden Gloves boxer. At five-foot-ten, 170 pounds, he could bring a load, which earned him the nickname "Boom Boom." He is still the most ferocious tackler and instinctive defensive back I've ever played with or saw during my coaching career.

Nevertheless, it was his character that impressed me the most. Most Sundays when I was at FSU, I attended mass at 5:30 p.m. College students always filled that mass, since it gave us a chance to sleep in. One day, while sitting around Coble Terrace, our football dorm, I asked Boom Boom, "I thought I saw you at mass last week. I thought you were Baptist." He said, "Joe, there are so many good-looking girls at that service, I have to go!"

Vintage Boom Boom.

Fast-forward to years later, and Brian was diagnosed with ALS. Like he did on the football field, he fought the disease and did so with a grace and class that inspired me to my core. He died in August of 2018.

Although we had a winning season in 1981 at 6–5, we were not invited to a bowl game. I had been redshirted that year, so my football life contained a lot of practice and no games. I didn't like sitting in the stands like any other student, so I couldn't wait for the 1982 season.

I joined the travel squad in 1982. Because I'd played a year of prep school and I'd been redshirted a year, I suddenly became one of the older guys on the team. I served as the backup free safety behind Brian McCrary, a spot he would hold for most of the next three seasons. During that training camp, several of my teammates started teasing me about being "Coach Wessel."

Part of that "Coach" moniker came from my football knowledge. The strategy of the game came easy to me, and I wasn't shy about sharing my enthusiasm for the game. My teammates must have seen something in me that I didn't. Of course, if you're undersized and slower than most, you better bring some heart and knowledge to the table if you ever dreamed of playing.

I did not play much in 1982. Most of when I did play that season came in mop-up duty. But I patiently continued to wait my turn. We went 8–3 that season with wins at Ohio State, at Miami, and at South Carolina. Our only three losses were against Pittsburgh, LSU, and Florida. The LSU game was a pivotal game in our season. Everybody projected the winner of that game to go the Orange Bowl and the loser to the Gator Bowl. LSU beat us up in a 55–21 defeat. West Virginia, led by quarterback Jeff Hostetler, awaited us in Jacksonville.

Hostetler would lead the New York Giants to a win over the Buffalo Bills in Super Bowl XXV in Tampa, but he didn't have that same magic against us in the Gator Bowl. We capped off that season with a 31–12 win over the Mountaineers, which earned us a No. 10 ranking in United Press International's Coaches' Poll.

Becoming a starter and earning a scholarship became an obsession. My single-mindedness took a toll on my grades, but I had a good spring practice in 1983. That summer, I went home to Miami to take a break from Tallahassee and football. However, I wasn't about to sit around that summer. I wanted to do everything in my power to prepare for my junior season.

Going home gave me a chance to train and reconnect with many of the Miami Dolphins players from years past. Earnie Rhone continued to help me a lot during this period, whether we were working out together or he was filling my ears with positive information and helpful hints. Jimmy Cefalo was also instrumental in sharing his ideas on how a wide receiver looked at things while I tried to cover him during one-on-one drills.

I also got to work out with Dan Marino and David Woodley, the Dolphins' quarterbacks. Somehow Marino had slipped to the Dolphins in the 1983 Draft. John Elway, Todd Blackledge, Jim Kelly, Tony Eason, and Ken O'Brien were all selected in the first round before the Dolphins stole Marino with the twenty-seventh pick of the first round. Nobody ever really determined why he slipped, though negative rumors always appear around the draft. His illustrious Hall of Fame career would begin that season, and I found myself working against him during my summer workouts.

In addition to covering Cefalo that summer, I got to cover Mark Duper and Mark Clayton, who were phenomenal speedsters and Hall of Fame-type receivers. David Shula was coaching wide receivers at that time, so he would be out there along with Mike, his brother who was a sophomore quarterback at Alabama. Being around those guys really helped me get better.

I had great focus that summer, and I give a lot of credit to the guys I trained with for helping me find that focus.

While I spent the bulk of my time working out, I landed a job at Sportrooms, a racquetball fitness center owned by Tim Foley, my childhood hero and a Dolphin workout partner. Tim told me to talk to the manager, Brian Scott. He didn't want to meet with me, but I insisted, so I went up and interrupted his lunch. You guessed it, he hired me. Little did Brian know that this new employee would soon change his life forever. That summer, I introduced him to my sister Margie, who worked as the head volleyball coach at Clemson University. Two years later, they were married at Saint Patrick's Church, the same church my grandfather Louis Wessel helped rebuild after the "Great Miami Hurricane" of 1926.

That summer also featured the moment I had been waiting for, when my parents received a letter that began as follows:

Dear Mr. and Mrs. Wessel,
Happy to inform you that your son has earned his scholarship for the calendar year 1983–84, he is a great asset to our family . . .

Coach Bowden's signature appeared at the bottom of the letter.

The fact they had waited until they did to give me the scholarship frosted me a little bit, detracting some from the joy of my accomplishment. However, I did understand why they handled the situation the way they did. If I'd gotten injured that spring, they would have wasted a scholarship on me. Business is business.

Bottom line, I had earned a scholarship. Given all I'd been through, that felt like a big deal. My parents had paid for three years of my schooling and one year of prep school. Freeing them from that financial burden felt very rewarding to me. Getting awarded a scholarship also validated eight years of training, running, lifting weights, and film study. Eight years of stress and anxiety on the long road of becoming a major college football player.

Earning that scholarship had been a definite peak in my life. Little did I know that a gorge sat dead ahead, but in the moment it felt truly great.

In typical fashion, Dad let me know how proud he was of my accomplishment and offered the appropriate remarks expressing that sentiment. He also made the statement that would become popular within our family when he told me, "Keep your eye on the bird."

The story he told featured a man looking down the barrel of a gun to shoot a bird. The man doesn't see the branches on the tree, he doesn't see the person behind the branches on the tree, and he doesn't see the building behind the tree. He focuses and stays locked in on the bird until he kills it. The message being, even at the height of things, I still couldn't take my foot off the gas pedal. "Keep your eye on the bird. You haven't shot it dead yet. Keep your focus. Eliminate the distractions."

Of course, Dad didn't just deliver the message with words. He also used a prop by employing an all-white cockatiel. I named the bird Yacob. Dad could be quirky with stuff. He'd give you anecdotes and thought processes, but his "Wesselisms" were classic. Not always direct, he often would relay a message through his story, or a song, or through the bird. The message in this case: Supreme athletes, or people who are extraordinary at anything they do, usually are single-minded in what they are and who they are. They don't have hobbies. It's what they do. Like the sharpshooter.

The bird's name came from one of Dad's favorite sayings, "Don't be a Yacob." Basically, this was Dad's way of saying, "Don't be a dumbass" or "Don't be stupid in your decisions." I don't know where the term came from, but I'm guessing it was a Yiddish term he heard growing up in Miami Beach.

Dad gave me that cockatiel and wrote me a note that he put in the bird cage when he gave me the bird. I took Yacob to FSU with me, and I had that bird for close to a year and a half. I carted Yacob back and forth from Tallahassee to South Florida during vacations. The bird definitely served a purpose. Every time I looked into that cage, I would be reminded about keeping my focus. Stupid, but simple. And it worked.

CHAPTER 11

Fired as a Junior

I RETURNED TO TALLAHASSEE FOR my junior season in the best shape of my life. I had gotten faster and stronger over the summer. I felt as though I had prepared myself to play in every sense. During two-a-days, they switched me from free safety to strong safety. Normally, the free safety had more speed than I did. A lot of people refer to the position as center field, because, like in baseball, the free safety roamed the center of the field and went to wherever trouble presented itself, whether that was helping a cornerback on either side of the field or handling what happened in the center of the field. A strong safety played closer to the line, and the position dealt more with contact and run responsibilities along with staying on the tight end.

That 1983 season also marked the year the coaches paired me up with a new roommate. He played wide receiver, he didn't have a roommate, and he was Jack Nicklaus's son.

Steve Nicklaus is the second oldest of the Nicklaus children, behind Jackie. Nan, Gary, and Michael followed him in that order.

Steve had been in Tallahassee since arriving in the fall of 1981 on scholarship from West Palm Beach Benjamin High School. When Steve first came to Tallahassee for a recruiting visit, what caught my eye, as well as everybody else's, was the fact that Jack walked onto the field with him. The Golden Bear in Tallahassee, wow! I'd been friendly with Steve during his freshman year, but we didn't have too much interaction. Steve could be difficult, and I'm sure he felt the same way about me. He was confident and, at times, a bit boisterous. Of course, we battled against each other every day at practice because I played in the secondary and he played receiver. We even talked a little trash . . . okay, we talked a lot of trash. I enjoyed his company, and I couldn't have asked for a better roommate.

Given Dad's love of golf, he offered a predictable response at the news about my new roommate: "You've got to be kidding me."

I met Jack after the first game of the 1983 football season. There were a lot of people hanging out in the apartment. Jack walked into the front room and grabbed me by the arm. He didn't bother to introduce himself before he guided me through twenty or so people to a back room. The first words out of his mouth were "How are you two getting along?" The question addressed my relationship with Steve. He obviously was genuinely concerned about his son and wanted to know if we had any issues. We had been roommates for just over a month, two weeks during which we were in training camp. We were still on our honeymoon!

"We're getting along fine," I told him, thinking, *What in the world is this all about?*

While initially I didn't understand what happened that night, that first meeting with Jack always stuck out to me. In retrospect, I realized that his thought process began with caring about his kids. That spoke volumes about how ingrained he was in his family life. I always admired that. My initial impression was reinforced the older I got when I heard the stories about Jack. I believe you learn to be that way. That's not something that comes naturally to everybody. For Jack, it probably dated back to his own upbringing.

Jack's father, Charlie, had been a pharmacist in Columbus, Ohio, and owned several Nicklaus Pharmacies. When Charlie broke his ankle early in Jack's life, he introduced his son to the sport while trying to rehabilitate from his injury. The rest is history.

I knew that Jack had vowed early in his professional career that, unless he had his wife and kids with him, he'd never be away from home for more than fourteen days in a row. Given the obligations and pursuits of a professional golfer, that's a tall order.

Jack credited his father for teaching him how to lose gracefully. Jack singled that out as the hardest lesson for a professional athlete to learn.

Charlie died of pancreatic cancer in 1970 at age fifty-six. In the aftermath of his father's death, Jack better understood how much his professional golf career had meant to his father. At that point, Jack rededicated himself to golf.

I had told Jack the truth the first time I met him. Steve's boisterous nature never bothered me. That was Steve being Steve. Even to this day, he still cuts me off. And he's quick to respond to something that he may not know anything about, but he will give you his opinion.

We enjoyed each other's company, we hung out, we played some golf, and we forged a lasting friendship.

Going up against each other in practice at times, Steve and I would bust balls. There's no question about that. Neither of us was getting a whole bunch of reps either, so a lot of times we were standing over on the side together. More times than not, he went up against the cornerbacks because he played wideout.

Steve had arrived at FSU far more heralded than I. Unfortunately for Steve, the guys in front of him were a solid group. Jesse Hester, Hassan Jones, Weegie Thompson, all of them played in the NFL.

I had a great camp that fall of 1983 after getting moved to strong safety. When they announced the starters to begin the season, the sheet read: Free safety—Brian McCrary, Strong safety—Joe Wessel. My persistence, hard work, and patience had paid off.

We opened the season in a night game at Doak Campbell Stadium on September 3 against East Carolina. A crowd of 46,261 fans witnessed perhaps the worst game of my life.

Though the Pirates lacked national recognition, they returned ten starters on offense and had great athletes and future NFL players throughout their roster. ECU ran the option, and their quarterback, Kevin Ingram, ran the offense masterfully. However, unlike many option quarterbacks, he was an equally proficient passer. After college, he played several years in the Canadian Football League. Their running back, Ernest Byner, went on to play fourteen years for the Cleveland Browns, Washington Redskins, and Baltimore Ravens. Their tight end, Norwood Vann, went on to play for the Rams and the Raiders. They also had All-American Terry Long, who was one of the most athletic offensive linemen I ever played against. He went on to play eight years for the Pittsburgh Steelers, then tragically ended his life in 2005.

ECU ran the "freeze option offense." That meant the quarterback took the snap, stepped back from the line of scrimmage, and froze, or paused. That pause gave the offensive guard (Long) the chance to pull while the tight end would down block, or arc block, outside. The fullback would run into the line of scrimmage, the quarterback would either give him the ball or fake it to him and continue down the line, running the option with the running back. He could keep the ball or make the pitch, based on how the defense reacted.

Since I played strong safety, my job called for me to read the tight end and see if he blocked down or arc blocked. Sometimes he would run a pass route instead, which mandated that I cover him. We had successfully practiced for the freeze option. You had to be disciplined with your assignments to stop this offense. And we were prepared in that respect. What you can't prepare for when playing an option attack, if you don't normally play teams that run the option, is the game speed of the option. You can't simulate the option team's game speed in practice. ECU's game speed proved to be so much faster than what we had practiced. Part of that could be attributed to the quality of their athletes.

They threw a bomb over my head off a play-action fake for a touchdown. Later in the game I had Byner one-on-one at the goal line, and he juked me so badly, I fell on my face. He then walked right into the end zone. Those two touchdowns earned me a trip to the principal's office—a phone call from defensive coordinator/defensive backs coach Jack Stanton, who sat in the press box. Stanton could be a ballbuster, and he fired me, telling me, "Get on the bench, and if you move, you'll never see the field again." That's how pissed off he was.

Nevertheless, we ended up beating East Carolina, 47–46. They were a good team that went 8–3. Their only losses that season were to FSU, Florida, and Miami by a total of fourteen points.

The next morning's *Tallahassee Democrat* featured a picture of our free safety and me chasing Norwood Vann. Seeing that picture wasn't the best way to start my day.

Stanton stood true to his word. I didn't see the field much for the remainder of that season.

The following week, we played No. 13 LSU in Baton Rouge, which was a big TV game. Leading up to the game, a headline read, "Defense Sees New Faces in the Lineup." Yet I was the only change. Man, that put me in a funk.

Still, I never thought about quitting. "Keep your eye on the bird." Dad's saying kept me focused.

Dad had always preached to finish what you were doing. In his eyes, you never started anything you weren't going to finish. Even if you were just doing yard work. I told Dad about my situation, and he tried to make sure I didn't lose my head. He told me time and again, "Keep your options open. You're going to make the right decision." My mother, with her athletic background, reinforced the message, as well.

Dad pushed me to gather all the information I could. That way I could make smart, rational decisions. Hasty decisions were the enemy. He'd tried to live his life using that philosophy and managed to ingrain that philosophy in me everything I did. Further, he told me, "In war, you can't make hasty decisions. You might have to make quick decisions, but think things out and be thoughtful in the decisions you make."

I think Dad understood Stanton's position because Dad adhered to discipline. Because of Dad, I accepted Stanton and respected him, since, in a way, he reminded me a lot of Dad. Both had nonverbal communication for me where positive reinforcement and acceptance were concerned.

Dad came up to two or three games. We talked every week. He continued to give me reinforcement, like, "Hang in there. This is what you've worked for, regardless. I know it hurts." That week-to-week conversation came even when we lost or I didn't get to play. He and my mother would put my situation into perspective.

Eventually, I managed to arrive at a positive outlook. In a letter to my parents dated October 25, 1983, I wrote the following:

> . . . I realized that football is not everything. I can't let it run my life like I've let it.

We finished with an 8–4 record, capping the season with a win over North Carolina in the Peach Bowl.

At the Peach Bowl, Pat Milligan, a starting defensive back who walked on with me in 1980, and I drummed up a deal. We planned for him to run off the field toward the end of the game and I would go in to take his place. I figured that would be the last play I ever played at FSU after what had transpired.

Then Jack Stanton got fired after the season and went to the Atlanta Falcons to coach under Dan Henning. I found that somewhat ironic. You get fired from a college job and you get hired as the secondary coach with the Falcons, an NFL team, which competes at a higher level of football. That just shows you how crazy coaching is.

I've come to realize that Jack had been ahead of his time and was probably better suited to coach in the NFL. Nobody was a better technician in relation to defensive backfield play.

Mickey Andrews was hired to be the new defensive coordinator/defensive backs coach, which completely changed my outlook and fortunes. I would have another chance. At least that's what I hoped for.

CHAPTER 12

Golfing with the Golden Bear's Son and White Fang

GOLF CAME BACK TO ME a little in high school, but mostly, my teenage years centered around team sports—football, basketball, and baseball, which didn't leave a lot of time for golf. Occasionally, I'd play a round with Dad when we were not in the Keys fishing or diving.

Once I moved to Tallahassee, the country club sports of tennis and golf started to pique my interest. Barry Voltapetti, one of the offensive linemen on the team, loved playing tennis as much as I did, so we would go and turn on the tennis court lights at local apartment buildings on Sunday evenings and play until the wee hours.

Sometimes I'd get invited to play golf, and in turn playing golf became a passion during my first summer at FSU.

The school golf course "Seminole" sat close to The Reservation, a lake that students frequented to go swimming, boating, or canoeing. In addition to being a great man, our athletic trainer, Don "Doc" Fauls, was an avid golfer. Once in a while, I would join him and his assistant trainer, Randy Oravetz, out at Seminole. Doc loved golf, loved to talk about the swing, and he was always willing to offer tips to enhance performance.

Doc remained open to helping rehab athletes from all sports, even professionals. Mark Lye, who played on the PGA Tour back then, would come to Tallahassee to get treatment from Doc. I wound up playing with Mark on several occasions and marveled at the consistency of the ball contact he made and the seemingly effortless swing. Mark's putting was impressive, too. He putted cross-handed, a style that I'd never before seen. Few professionals putted cross-handed back then, though a lot of professionals use the cross-handed approach today. I guess the success I saw Mark have while putting cross-handed made an impression on me, because I've been putting cross-handed ever since. What stood out most from watching Mark play was how he could recover from bad shots. It seemed like no trouble could prevent him from making par. He could get up and down from a water fountain. Playing with him taught me just how good professional golfers were. Mark could seemingly do anything he wanted to do on the golf course, yet he finished with just one career win on the PGA Tour—the Bank of Boston Classic on September 11, 1983.

Eventually, I had the opportunity to play whenever I wanted to at the FSU course. I started to get the itch the more I played and the better I got.

The first time I played a round with Steve Nicklaus was at the FSU course. Unsurprisingly, Steve played like you would have thought the son of Jack Nicklaus would play. He could shoot 74 or 75 without ever breaking a sweat. The things he could do with a golf ball weren't things guys my age could do. He could draw a ball, do whatever he wanted with it. And the way he made contact, you could tell he was different. He could crush a golf ball. It was scary.

I recall thinking, *Geez, if I could ever play golf like that, I'd never step onto a football field.* But you had to understand Steve's confident personality. He came off as, "I don't need golf. That's easy." Having his own unique identity seemed to be his cause, which perhaps was why he played football. God knows what he could have done if he'd played on the PGA Tour, because he was probably one of the better athletes in their family. He stood six-foot-two. He wasn't six-four like his brother Jackie, but he wasn't small like brother Gary, who stood five-ten. Gary went on to play golf at Ohio State like his father, before he turned professional in 1991.

I'd bet if Steve had to do it all over again, he would have played golf and tried to make that his profession.

To Steve's credit, when you played with him, he wasn't out there just screwing around. It's been my experience playing with talented golfers like Steve that often they act indifferent about what they shoot. Not Steve. He maintained a competitive nature, though he wasn't some hotheaded golf brat, either. You'd never see him throw or break his clubs. Steve just wanted to whip your ass on the golf course, just as the rest of us do.

We'd play as much as our schedule would allow.

Whether I played with Steve or others, golf started to become a big part of my life. I began playing more with Dad on vacations and breaks from school.

When I accidently threw and broke my Ping putter, Steve took care of me. That's what roommates do.

"Here, use this one," he told me, handing over a Bull's Eye putter that looked beat up and had white paint flaking off it. Anybody who has ever played golf understands how old clubs wind up in the garage. In that respect, I could only imagine how many old clubs the Nicklaus family had floating around in their garage. Based on that fact, I didn't feel particularly beholden to Steve's offering, nor did I attach any real significance to that moment—at least not initially.

I never felt comfortable with that putter the few times I played with it, and I quickly stopped using it. Technology upgrades during that time made the ball come off the putter cleaner and with less shock to the hands. To me, the football player, that Bull's Eye felt like a butter knife on the end of a stick. Plus, that Bull's Eye looked like an old putter, so that wasn't cool! I had no idea that the putter was close to twenty years old. Nor did I know that flat stick had a glorious past, a future to be determined, and a famous name: White Fang!

CHAPTER 13

Block That Kick!

MICKEY ANDREWS'S ARRIVAL TO FSU as the defensive coordinator/ defensive backs coach after the 1983 season meant everything to me.

Mickey had a unique way about him. He'd bust your balls, then he'd come back and put his arm around you when you were walking off the field. He had a good football mind, and he knew how to motivate kids. But he also brought a hell of a lot of personality to the job—an element that showed he cared about you. It's not that Jack Stanton didn't care about you, but he represented the old guard. Mickey signaled the transition to the new guard. He'd ask, "Hey, did you break up with your girlfriend? Do you have a test? What's going on? You don't seem like you're into it."

He'd been an all-around athlete, playing center field on the University of Alabama baseball team and he'd been an All-American defensive back and wide receiver on two of Bear Bryant's National Championship football teams. He just brought a different feel to the defense.

Mickey wasn't floored by our level of talent when he reached FSU.

Coach Bowden had told Mickey that he wanted to simplify the defense by using one defensive front and one coverage throughout spring practice. Coach Bowden's intention was to get better by stressing fundamentals. That philosophy fit Mickey perfectly. He always believed that the game of football was not so much about the X's and the O's as it was about the players.

Plus, where Mickey was concerned, everybody started with a clean slate when he began his new position as defensive coordinator.

Mickey said recently, "Sometimes when you make a change, defensive coordinator, defensive back coach, whatever, it gives a guy new life so to speak. I think Joe just needed a chance. Just needed to know that somebody really cared about him and was more interested in him for more than just being a football player. With that opportunity that he was given, it just kind of clicked for him."

Mickey and I really did click. Recently, he told Bill Chastain about what he'd seen in me when he arrived in Tallahassee:

"Joe reminded me of me when I was playing ball. He wasn't going to overwhelm you with his size or his strength. Basically, he was just a slow white guy who had only one speed, and that was wide open. You knew you were going to get that every play. He was consistent with it. One of the main things that Joe and I connected on was the effort and the intensity that he played with."

After all, max effort had been ingrained in me thanks to Dad. I knew I wasn't fast, and the only thing that I could control was how hard I played. Use my brain with what speed I did have. I wasn't going to run a 4.5 forty-yard dash. If I had run a 4.5 or 4.4, I could have taken a wrong step and still made it up. That's the same thing as somebody doing it the right way and not having to make up. It was nice that Mickey recognized that.

Mickey was just one of those guys—he was honest. Maybe he did see something in me that he saw in himself. Initially, he probably buried me after watching film from the previous year. I'm sure

Chuck Amato and Coach Bowden were telling him about the hold-overs on defense. I probably fell into the categories of "You know, he can't play" or "He just hasn't done it."

Mickey might have liked my effort, but when I finished spring practice prior to my senior season, my name could be found in the fifth spot for free safety.

We didn't even have a fifth-team depth chart when I first got to FSU.

Coach Bowden to this day makes the claim he figured I'd make a visit to his office before the start of my senior season and tell him that I was quitting, that I'd decided I was just going to get my degree, yet I can honestly say quitting never crossed my mind. I had another semester of school. I knew I had to take twenty-one hours to graduate. I reckoned that I'd done the football thing for four years, so why not stick it out and see what happens?

Thank God I didn't quit. One guy got hurt, another came back out of shape, and a guy flunked out. They were forced to use me. At first, I only played on the punt-block team. Then a need arose for somebody to fill the nickelback in our nickel defense, which is a defense that uses five defensive backs instead of four. I backed my way into winning that nickelback job.

I had the best 10-yard times on the team, but one of the slowest 40-yard times for a defensive back. Being quick for ten yards helped me block punts, as I could get off the line and accelerate.

From the outset of fall practice, I went out early before practice with the punters and kickers. I'd line up, and when the center snapped the football, I'd start running. My goal was to get as far past the punter as I could. I told our punter, "Look, I'm not going to block the punt. Don't mind me."

I would just sprint toward the punter on most every snap. That's all I would do—practice that. Once we started doing some things live at practice, the coaches started noticing what I could do. Next thing I knew, I found myself on the starting punt return team for all the two-a-day practices.

I would study centers prior to the game when the punters and kickers went out early. Our deep snapper was J.D. Dowell from Tampa. I learned to get jumps, like a base stealer against a pitcher. I thought of it as a nine-and-one-half-yard dash. The punter lined up around fourteen to fifteen yards behind the line of scrimmage, and the goal was for me to get airborne at nine-and-a-half yards. I needed to cover that distance in about 1.7 seconds. Speed helped, but instincts were more important. I'd cut across the punter's face and try to penetrate as far as I could in the time that it took him to get off the kick. I got used to doing that, and I had a knack for it. On field goals, I mapped out steps—one, two, three, get in the air. I guess I had a knack for blocking kicks, too.

Mickey said that he arrived at FSU and stressed that one of the ways that they were going to get better was in the area of blocking kicks.

"Joe just had a knack for getting off the ball, like people talk about base stealers in baseball," Mickey told Bill. "You have to find something in there that's going to give you an advantage if you don't have great speed. And he was like that. He would really study the films and look at the snappers. Any little mannerism or twitch that he could gain an advantage on. That's what he did.

"Also, he was wide open just about on that first step. It was something that he could help the team with and he was amazing at that time, how many kicks he blocked in his career. And he never lined up more than a foot from the line of scrimmage. It's crazy how many blocks he had that year. That really helped us win some games that season."

My efforts paid off. As the backup safety, I became the No. 1 nickelback in passing situations, and I ended up starting two games at free safety when Brian McCrary got hurt. We played a lot of zone defense and didn't play a lot of man-to-man. When I did have to cover somebody, I normally found myself covering a tight end or a running back coming out of the backfield. Rarely did I find myself one-on-one with a wideout.

We won our first four games of my senior season in 1984, against East Carolina, Kansas, Miami, and Temple. The first blocked punt of my career came in our 48–17 win over East Carolina, and it led to a touchdown. My second came in the next game, a 42–16 win over Kansas. Bruce Heggie grabbed that one and returned it for a touchdown.

Both of my blocks were somewhat unheralded by the media. The *Tallahassee Democrat* ran a photo of the one against East Carolina, but the caption identified me—the guy who blocked the kick—as Mike Lively, a reserve kicker on the team.

Following the Kansas game, the Associated Press credited Joe Russell as the player who blocked the punt. Even the scoreboard got it wrong, spelling my name WESSAL.

After that, it became a running joke on the team. I told teammates that I'd become the Rodney Dangerfield of college football, getting no respect.

Playing against Miami in the Orange Bowl in our third game of the season brought a special thrill. I'd spent a lot of time in that old stadium. My family and a lot of friends came to that one, and, even better, we won, 38–3.

We played Temple in the fourth game, and I blocked a field goal and a punt. On the field goal, Eric Riley picked it up and scored.

We were one of the first teams to have practice on Monday nights, but it made sense. Waiting until Monday night, rather than Monday afternoon, gave the coaches an opportunity to do more of the playbook and the scouting report on Monday afternoon. Then we'd practice on Monday night at Doak Campbell.

In contrast to Coach Bowden, Mickey Andrews could be very emotional.

Coach Bowden dropped two F-bombs within earshot of me in five years. When Mickey first arrived, F-bombs spewed from his mouth a mile a minute, which didn't exactly jive with the rule in Coach Bowden's playbook prohibiting cussing on the field. We were 4–0 and headed to Memphis for our next game against Memphis State and were in the midst of our regularly scheduled Monday night practice when Mickey, with a dip secure in his mouth, yelled, "Eric Riley, there's scouts out here and you're out here f***ing around."

Right away, we saw Coach Bowden start toward our group. We began giggling around Mickey, because we were like, "You're in trouble now." And we always laughed about the differences between Mickey and Coach Bowden. Mickey came into a different environment than he'd been in in the NFL and the USFL, where cussing had been commonplace. But at FSU, Mickey's cussing didn't sit well with Coach Bowden. Mickey got the message and changed his tune over time.

Going to Memphis for the game against Memphis State afforded me an opportunity to pay it forward. St. Jude's Children Hospital always had a special place in my heart, since that's the place where John Stack spent the final months of his life. To honor John, I wanted to visit St. Jude's on that trip. I approached Reverend Ken Smith and our strength coach, Dave Van Halanger, who were both active in the Fellowship of Christian Athletes organization, and they helped facilitate that happening.

Six of us visited the hospital including Eric Riley, Eric Thomas, Jerry Riopelle, Louis Berry, and Parrish Barwick. We took a bunch of posters and t-shirts to give to the kids. As soon as we got there, a nurse took us aside and said, "You're going to see things that are not tasteful. We just take things a day at a time here." When she said that, it really hit us. That was our whole theme that year—one down at a time. That visit did more for me than anything we did for the kids we visited. Such a visit can really bring you back to earth.

Unfortunately, we tied with Memphis State, 17–17. The following week, we played in front of the home crowd at Doak Campbell Stadium, and we lost a 42–41 heartbreaker to Auburn.

This tough loss set the stage for our next game, on November 3, 1984, when we traveled to Sun Devil Stadium in Tempe, Arizona, to play Arizona State. It was there that I made perhaps my greatest impact on the football field.

We fell behind, 17–0, before most of the crowd of 68,754 had arrived, but we cut the deficit to 20–17 by halftime. I accounted for one of the scores in the second quarter when Lenny Chavers blocked a punt. I picked up the ball at the 8-yard line and ran it into the end zone for our first touchdown. In the fourth quarter, I blocked a punt at the 34-yard line and scored my second touchdown, putting us up, 52–30, a lead we would not relinquish. My two touchdowns on blocked punts tied the NCAA record for the most blocked punts for touchdowns in a game.

We were disappointed when we finished our schedule with a 7–3–1 record, but we were still Bowl-bound. We earned an invitation to play the University of Georgia in the Citrus Bowl on December 22, 1984.

Prior to the Citrus Bowl, I graduated with a marketing and business degree. When I walked across the stage during the commencement ceremony, my family and friends hollered, "Block that kick!" A photo of me hugging Dad ran in the *Tallahassee Democrat* the following day. In the photo, you can see the sign hanging from my back that I wore to graduation. It read: "Dad, I made it. I ♥ ya Wessel Clan!"

In later years, Dad would comment on how proud he was to have all three children graduate from college. Mine took a little longer. Nonetheless, I walked across the stage that day. A week later, I would experience my final football game as a player in Orlando at the Citrus Bowl and an opportunity to make Dad and the rest of the Wessel clan proud once again. Lucky for me, I was a part of FSU's special teams unit, which had an amazing knack to produce results. During that regular season alone, we had blocked eight punts and returned six for touchdowns. What we did came to be known as the "FSU Block Party."

Oftentimes, a block came down to a mixture of things, like getting the jump on the center. Most of my blocks didn't come on their first punt. Instead, we'd talk on the sidelines about the weak spots in their line. Sometimes I could see the panic in the punter's eyes. Those were the guys who normally rushed their kicks because they knew we could block punts. Normally, guys who punted for big averages did not get off good punts against us.

Yet the game against Georgia was no cakewalk. After all, Georgia had the hands-down best placekicker in college football in Kevin Butler. He'd go on the next year to be an integral part of the Chicago Bears, who stormed to the Super Bowl and crushed the Patriots. Butler had such a powerful leg that Georgia would be in field goal range any time they got close to midfield. He'd kicked seventy-eight field goals during his career, including a 60-yarder that season that had beaten Clemson on the final play of the game.

The Citrus Bowl had a sellout crowd for the game that was shown to a national television audience. We were down, 14–0, at the half and still trailed, 17–9, with just under four minutes to go when Georgia had to punt.

I didn't think about the fact that the final minutes of my days playing football were about to tick off the scoreboard, and I tried not to focus on the fact that every time Georgia had to kick in that game, my family held up a sign in the stands that read: "Block That Kick Wessel."

In fact, they were still waiving that sign when Georgia lined up

Dad at fifteen years old with his mom, Esther, in February 1942. WWII awaits!

Dad during World War II, perhaps on the lookout for the enemy (circa 1942–43)?

Chuck Zink presenting trophies to me and my sister Margie circa late 1960s.

John Stack and Joe Wessel at graduation day, Pace High School, Miami, Florida, May 1979.

Old man of the Sea! Dad with two of his best friends!

Dad and I on #13 East at Oak Hill Country Club, Rochester, New York, circa 1991.

Photo with Coach Bowden freshman year. 1981 Orange Bowl: FSU vs. Oklahoma.

My senior year of FSU football was one of the most memorable years from my college tenure (August 1984).

Philadelphia Eagles game day in 1997. Here I am, getting the players pumped up!

The day I met Jack Nicklaus for the first time, 1983.

Jack taking back possession of his $1 million putter on April 12, 2003.

Hole	Member Tees	Masters Tees	Par	Handicap Rating	JACK	STEVE	DAD	JOE	Hole	Member Tees	Masters Tees	Par	Handicap Rating	JACK	STEVE	DAD	JOE
1	365	435	4	9	6	5	5	5	10	450	495	4	6	5	5	7	5
2	500	575	5	1	5	6	6	7	11	375	490	4	12	4	5	6	5
3	340	350	4	11	4	③	5	4	12	145	155	3	16	3	3	7	6
4	170	205	3	15	3	4	5	3	13	455	510	5	4	6	5	7	6
5	400	455	4	5	4	4	5	4	14	380	440	4	8	4	5	6	5
6	165	180	3	17	3	②	4	3	15	475	500	5	2	5	5	7	5
7	320	410	4	13	4	5	6	5	16	145	170	3	18	3	4	5	5
8	460	570	5	3	5	5	6	④	17	350	425	4	14	4	5	6	5
9	380	460	4	7	5	5	5	4	18	375	465	4	10	5	4	6	5
Out	3100	3640	36		39	39	47	39	In	3150	3650	36		39	41	57	47
									Total	6250	7290	72		78	80	104	86

HANDICAP

Scorer

Attest   Date 10/22/03

Net Scores

Distances as shown represent yardage from tee markers to the mid point of the green.

If I had stopped playing after nine holes . . . I could've always said I tied the six-time Masters champ! October 22, 2003.

Papa Joe and The Golden Bear are all smiles before dinner at Augusta National.

Jack exchanged the $20 for a $10 bill . . . with a little extra!

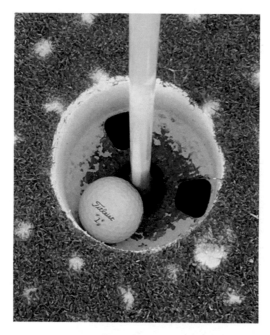

Hole-in-one at Oak Hill CC in October 2017 . . . The aforementioned "Titleist #1."

Top left—White Fang in its final resting place in the Jack Nicklaus Museum, Columbus, Ohio.

Photos courtesy of Joe Wessel.

to punt. We ran a play called "Block 10." Ten defenders rushed the punter, five on each side. Stretching the protection was the principle of the play. In theory, if we overloaded the pressure outside, the opposing team stretched its protection outside, which opened holes on the inside. And vice versa if we overloaded the pressure inside.

Georgia adjusted to the left outside, which opened a hole on the inside of the line.

Our nose guard, Lenny Chavers, broke through the middle of the Bulldogs' line to block Chip Andrews's punt. I'd been lined up on the right side and had been close to the punter, but Lenny got there first. The ball ricocheted off Lenny and went backward. I scooped it up at the 14-yard line, then scooted into the end zone to cut the lead to 17–15. That gave us nine blocked kicks for the season, setting an NCAA record.

We went for two points.

Coach Bowden had a reputation for trick plays, and what we ran personified that reputation. Our quarterback, Eric Thomas, took the snap, then pitched the ball to the right toward our tailback, Tony Smith. Before the ball got to Tony, Darrin Holloman, our wide receiver, grabbed the pitch and headed in the other direction. Darrin split two defenders to get into the end zone to tie the game.

Our sideline went berserk, but we had to regroup to finish off the game. Plenty of time remained on the clock, particularly since they had a weapon in Butler's powerful right leg.

Neither team could get anything going in the next two possessions. Then Georgia began a drive with less than two minutes to go. At this point, their quarterback, James Jackson, looked down the field and tried to connect with his wide receiver, Jimmy Hockaday. Fortunately for us—and me—Hockaday couldn't make the catch. The ball went right through his hands and directly to me, allowing me to make my first career interception.

That gave us a chance to get something going on offense and

possibly win the game. Instead, we sputtered and had to punt back to Georgia with 21 seconds to go. Jackson tried two deep passes that fell incomplete. I couldn't believe what happened next. With seven seconds left on the clock, Georgia coach Vince Dooley sent out Butler to try a field goal. In hindsight, Georgia probably should have tried something short to get Butler a little closer. For some reason they didn't, leaving a lot of real estate between Butler's big foot and the goal post.

Butler looked as though he'd lost something in the grass while searching for the perfect spot to have his kicking tee placed on the Orlando Stadium's turf. (Back in those days, college kickers could use a tee on field goals.) He finally settled on a spot between their 39- and 38-yard lines, which meant he'd be trying a 71-yard field goal. If he made the kick, Butler would have set a record for the longest field goal in college football history. Having seen Butler kick, I knew that the prospect of him making the kick wasn't totally out of the realm of reality. He'd nailed one from 72 yards during pre-game warmups. If Georgia's all-time greatest kicker—a distinction he owns today—made the improbable kick, Georgia would walk off the field with a 20–17 win.

Butler's foot blistered the football, which seemed to explode before arching high and straight up the field toward the goal post.

I thought he'd made the kick. He'd made such good contact with the football, but ultimately it fell just short, allegedly landing two or three yards shy of the crossbar. Amazing.

Later, I heard that Butler had tried to put a little more arch on his kick to avoid the possibility of having us block his kick.

Final score: FSU 17, Georgia 17.

Given where we'd come from, that tie felt like a win to us. And given where I'd come from, I couldn't have scripted a better way to end my career. The spring before, our coaches had told me I needed to do something special, or better than anybody else, if I dreamed of setting foot on the field. I managed to do so with my ability to block kicks. All told, I blocked four punts and a field goal that season, and I scored four touchdowns.

Coach Bowden recently told Bill Chastain: "Joe Wessel became a legend at FSU. He led the nation in blocked punts. You can't hardly find a guy who can block a punt. . . . His last year, he might have been the team's most valuable player."

NBC interviewed me after the game while Dad and Mom weaved their way down to the field to give me a hug amid a bunch of reporters. Jack Nicklaus stood next to the door to our locker room. The Golden Bear shook my hand and congratulated me on the game, the season, and graduating. He also gave me the keys to his Park City, Utah, townhouse to use on the skiing trip I made with college friends, which became a yearly ritual. We stayed at his house at Country Club of the Rockies a couple of years later. That experience marked the first time I saw a big screen TV in a house. Remember, this was the 1980s, so it was a rear projection model.

I guess that was one of the perks, or opportunities, of being Jack Nicklaus's son's roommate.

CHAPTER 14

Coaching Decision

DURING MY FINAL SEASON AT FSU, I began to entertain the idea of becoming a football coach. Heck, my teammates had already been calling me "Coach."

I'd gained so much knowledge over the years, the prospect seemed like part of a natural progression. I'd defended Mark Duper and Mark Clayton. I'd backpedaled with Tim Foley. I'd intercepted Dan Marino's and David Woodley's passes. Earl Morrall had been my first quarterback coach. I'd been around Don Shula, Howard Schnellenberger, and Bill Arnsparger. I also had experiences from playing high school, prep school, and college football.

Looking outside of sports also occurred to me. My degree from Florida State opened doors, and I had a nice offer from Proctor and Gamble to sell Citrus Hills Orange Juice and Folgers Coffee in Fort Lauderdale for $17,500 a year. A company car came in the deal, along with a $500 expense account.

Despite the nice offer, I continued to think, *I have this football experience, why wouldn't I want to stay in it and try to make career out of it?* I'd been in that arena for a decade. Dad told me I should pursue what I wanted to do. He had a staunch belief in people fulfilling their dreams. He also offered feedback while I weighed my decision.

Since Dad didn't have a coaching or football background, I think he could look at my situation more objectively. I knew the football side, but he asked questions about the business side of the job and the life I'd lead. What would the job do to me? What were the upsides and the downsides? Dad's feedback proved instrumental to making my decision. I decided that I absolutely wanted to go into coaching, a profession I felt I'd be passionate about. I just needed a job. I kept an open mind about where I wanted to go.

Mickey Andrews liked the idea of me going into coaching, too.

"I thought [Joe] would be a good coach," Mickey said recently. "He understood football. He had a good football mind. He was a smart guy. You just felt like he could be a teacher. He could teach. He could motivate."

Following our 17–17 tie with Georgia in the Citrus Bowl, Vince Dooley walked alongside me when I left the stadium after the game. The famed Georgia coach, who knew I had just graduated, asked, "What are you going to do?"

FSU linebackers coach Gene McDowell had just become the head coach at the University of Central Florida, and Arnsparger held the head coach position at LSU. Both offered me opportunities. I told Coach Dooley about those opportunities, prompting him to yell to Ray Goff, one of his assistants and the man who succeed him as Georgia's head coach following the 1988 season, "You make sure Joe comes back by to see us because I want him to be one of our GA's."

"Great," I said. "I'll come by."

I stopped in Athens, Georgia, on my way to Baton Rouge. They interviewed me for one of their graduate assistant jobs, but they were on the quarter system, so they couldn't get me into school in time. LSU could. Plus, Arnsparger was a defensive guy, and I had a Dolphins connection with him. He'd coached under Shula from 1970 to 1973 and from 1976 to 1983. I also had my mother's connection from her card games with B.J. Arnsparger.

My gut told me I needed to be at LSU, so I chose to be a graduate assistant making $7,500 a year, meaning I'd go to graduate school and coach football in Baton Rouge.

As I embarked on a coaching career, Steve Nicklaus began his working career, also. We stayed in touch and from time to time would see each other when I would come home for vacations. I even remember one time bringing Dad with me to play with Steve at Loxahatchee Club, which Jack had just built.

Grad assistant work is hard. You're not making much money, and you work to please and impress in hopes that you will get the chance one day to become a "full-timer." As bad as those first two years were, though, I knew I loved coaching, so I stuck with it.

CHAPTER 15

Looking for Work and Finding a Girl

Chuck Amato, who had been a coach at FSU, told me, "When you get in the coaching business, it's a job like any other job."

I would come to discover that as a player, you don't see things like you do when you are a coach. Because as a player you play or practice, and then you go back to school. You might have an hour meeting from time to time, then you would go home. A coach goes and watches more film after practice. A player tries to absorb strategy with little input. When you're a coach, you're trying to invent a strategy and get it ingrained into your players.

Bill Arnsparger turned over special teams to me my second year, and I helped the defensive backs coach, Mike Archer.

I have a lot to thank Coach Arnsparger for, since he gave me my first job forty-five days after I played my last college football game. The reality is that his wife, B.J., picked the graduate assistants out of the résumés that they had. I guess all the bridge nights that my mother shared with B.J. over the years helped me get my foot in the door.

Coach Arnsparger pushed me and gave me opportunities, advice, and often a hard time. He would write down everything in a spiral-bound notebook—a very detail-oriented man. Bill coached from 1950 to 1994, forty-four years of service and leadership to young men and to the game of football.

We won a Southeastern Conference Championship under Coach Arnsparger in 1986 and earned a spot in the Sugar Bowl against Nebraska.

To that point, LSU had gone 0–3 in bowl games with Coach Arnsparger at the helm. Going into this game, we were ranked No. 5, and Nebraska came in at No. 6. It was the third time in five seasons that the two teams had met in a bowl game. Nebraska had won all three games.

Adding to the storyline for that Sugar Bowl, Coach Arnsparger announced after our final game of the regular season against Tulane that he would be leaving LSU to become the athletic director at the University of Florida.

Sitting next to Coach Arnsparger on the bus before that Sugar Bowl game gave me my favorite memory of him. We talked about life, football, the upcoming game, and our futures—his as the Florida athletic director and mine as a full-time coach. I wished him good luck at Florida. I also told him that I could never root for the Gators.

We lost that bowl game, 30–15, and Bill moved on but continued to be my mentor and friend.

LSU selected the defensive coordinator, Mike Archer, to follow Coach Arnsparger as the head coach. Since we had just won LSU's first SEC championship since 1970, the administration thought the best course of action would be to hire from within the staff to maintain continuity in the program.

Mike's leadership skills were far different from Bill's. Mike was carefree and engaging to everyone. He kept things light and very loose. He had great rapport with his players.

That's when I got my first full-time job coaching the inside linebackers. Two years later, I coached the defensive backs. We had winning seasons in Archer's first two seasons as the head coach, including an SEC championship in 1988.

Nevertheless, LSU had losing seasons in 1989 and 1990, prompting the school to fire Archer and his staff—including me—with two games to go in the 1990 season. In the coaching business, you're only as good as your last championship. I became a member of John Gruden's fictitious club, the FFCA—Fired Football Coaches Association.

I wanted my parents to hear from me before the news reached Florida. I called Dad and confirmed the rumors. I told him I needed to find a job. Then jokingly I asked him if he needed a partner. Though we both laughed, that wasn't the last time that we would discuss that possibility.

During my period of unemployment, I became a "professional" golfer—at least that's what I teased. Since I still had a contract with LSU that paid me through July of 1991, I played golf every day in Baton Rouge while I looked for my next job. Didn't that constitute being a professional?

Following a golf game, fate entered my life at Superior Grill in Baton Rouge on a Thursday night in February of 1991.

While talking to a friend, I noticed a striking woman as she walked by. Upon her return, she passed us, and I pointed her out to Mike Clegg, my friend who was an LSU booster. Mike said, "You want to meet her?"

I responded quickly, "You bet."

Through Mike's introduction, we joined the table where she sat along with seven or eight women. We remained at their table the rest of the night.

I had an instant attraction to Mary Gayle Hamilton.

After talking at the table, we talked more in her car. I learned that Mary Gayle's mom had cancer and was not doing well, so she was going through a tough time in her life.

We went out about a week later, sharing dinner at a bar. The next morning I left beignets, coffee, and flowers at her door, along with a note that explained the beignets and coffee were for her and the flowers were for her mom. She'd said that she couldn't find the right guy. She didn't like the way most guys treated girls. She wanted to find a Southern Gentleman. That made the last line of my note easy:

Chivalry is not dead!

We began dating regularly while I continued to look for work.

Since Dad was the singer and the creative one in the family, and Mary Gayle was an interior designer and completely creative, they hit it off immediately when they first met. Two peas in a pod. Dad wasn't a man of many words, but the wink and the smirk told me he approved. They would always have something special between them.

At least my personal life appeared to have a future at that point, even if my professional life didn't seem so promising. I couldn't find a job. I didn't have a lot of coaching friends because the LSU job had been my first, and I stayed there six years. My situation caused me to think about whether I should stay in coaching.

I interviewed with Jackie Sherrill, who had just accepted the head coaching job at Mississippi State, and Bill Belichick, who just became the head coach of the Cleveland Browns. I didn't get either job, and at this point it was almost May.

Looking outside the box, I tried everything to find coaching jobs, and I even considered jobs not within the coaching ranks. That prompted me to reach out to Jack Nicklaus.

I'd always had a good relationship with Jack, so I called him and told him my situation.

He'd just opened up Golden Bear Sports Management, an endeavor that also included Steve. We talked, and they were interested in hiring me. I felt as though I'd found a perfect fit if I was going to get out of coaching. But my heart told me I wanted to remain on the sideline.

I also considered going to work with my father. After all, Dad had been a successful businessman and now was on his own as a food broker.

I wrote to Dad, telling him how I admired what he'd done in the food service business and that if I could learn the business from him, I would look forward to it. Dad considered my proposition but expressed to me his opinion that he thought I might be better served by continuing to chase my dream. His advice reinforced what my heart and gut were telling me to do—stay in coaching.

The only way at that time to stay in coaching was to volunteer at a top program like USC, Oklahoma, or Notre Dame.

Notre Dame had hired Gary Darnell to be its defensive coordinator prior to the 1990 season. He'd been the interim head coach at the University of Florida in 1989, and before that the Gators' defensive coordinator. Bill Arnsparger had been the Florida athletic director, so Gary knew Coach Arnsparger. And via a Coach Arnsparger connection, I got an interview at Notre Dame in May. They offered me the last open volunteer position on head coach Lou Holtz's staff!

I talked to Dad about the offer. Being Catholic, both of us had always dreamed about me going to Notre Dame. Keeping emotion out of the conversation, Dad assumed the voice of reason, presenting different considerations regarding the job. An important question for me pertained to how coaching would affect my relationship with Mary Gayle. He definitely could relate to my concern, but he reminded me, as he often did, to keep my priorities in order. Dad also asked me questions about the people I'd be with at Notre Dame. "What's Coach Holtz like? Who are the other coaches?" Dad wanted to be objective and present some of the possible pitfalls, but deep down we both knew this was an opportunity of a lifetime.

South Bend became the next stop.

CHAPTER 16

Notre Dame

EMOTIONALLY, I FELT LOW WHEN I left for South Bend. That changed once I arrived on campus in late May when I met with Coach Holtz shortly after spring practice.

Coach had landed the Notre Dame job prior to the 1986 season, after serving stints around the NFL and college football scene. The Fighting Irish were struggling when he took over the program, but that would change under his watch.

While Coach Holtz carried a ribbon-thin frame, wore glasses, and had a personality that most found interesting and funny, he insisted on discipline, and he was a taskmaster. Prior to his first season, he stressed the importance of team. Hoping to drive that concept home, he had the names removed from the backs of the players' jerseys.

After posting a 5–6 season his first year in South Bend, Coach Holtz's Irish improved dramatically, posting a 12–0 record during the 1988 season before defeating West Virginia in the Fiesta Bowl to become National Champions.

When I sat down with Coach Holtz, he told me, "Look Joe, if you help us this year, I'll help you get a job next year."

That eased my mind.

After I left Coach Holtz, I went into Gary Darnell's office. We talked about an hour, then he said, "Let's get out of here." Next thing you know, I was at Knollwood Country Club. I'm like, *Man this is cool.* I walked to the driving range and found Ara Parseghian hitting balls. I introduced myself to the famed former Notre Dame coach and thought about the letter I'd received from Notre Dame back in 1979 that wished me luck but told me I couldn't go to school there. That became my opening sentence on booster speaking engagements. "I wasn't smart enough to go to Notre Dame, but I'm smart enough to coach here."

I knew I needed to be at Notre Dame. My instincts just told me it would be the right place for me.

Among the items I'd packed to take with me to South Bend were a bunch of wooden-shafted clubs that Dad had given me. White Fang rested among that collection of clubs and made the trip. I put those clubs on a shelf, never unwrapped them, and never thought about them. In hindsight, it's amazing I did not get rid of them, because you certainly couldn't play with those clubs anymore.

While working as a volunteer at Notre Dame, I collected approximately $200 a week via unemployment. Meanwhile, I buried myself in my work. I think I received more respect for being a volunteer coach than I did for being a graduate assistant in my previous role!

Meanwhile, my relationship with Mary Gayle grew serious, even though she remained in Baton Rouge. Her mom passed away before I left for South Bend, so that spring she continued working and taking care of the family business.

My first season at Notre Dame started well for the team. We compiled an 8–1 record with wins over USC, Pitt, Michigan State, and Stanford. Our only loss heading into a game against No. 13 Tennessee came against Michigan in the second week. We felt pretty good hosting the Volunteers in South Bend on November 9, 1991. A lot of people were touting us as potential National Champions.

Unfortunately, our season began to unravel at that point.

After taking a 31–14 halftime lead, we had the worst collapse in the second half that I had ever experienced.

Our All-American punter/kicker, Craig Hentrich, sprained his right knee when Tennessee blocked his field goal attempt with fourteen seconds remaining in the second quarter. That block turned into an eighty-five-yard touchdown return and left the kicking duties up to a sophomore walk-on, Rob Leonard, which proved to be a critical development regarding the game's outcome.

Tennessee took their first and only lead of the game with just over four minutes to play. They correctly anticipated a blitz and scored on a twenty-six-yard screen pass, putting them up, 35–34.

Still, we had a chance to win, starting a drive at our 25 with 3 minutes and 57 seconds left on the clock. The offense came through, driving the ball to the Tennessee nine-yard line. With four seconds remaining, Leonard tried his first career college field goal.

The kick left his foot and deflected off the backside of one of Tennessee's charging defenders, causing the ball to miss wide right. We lost, 35–34.

After the game, Coach Holtz expressed disappointment by saying, "I've been in this game a long time. That was as difficult a loss as I've been associated with, ever. Ever."

Our troubles continued the next week, when we traveled to Happy Valley and lost to Penn State, 35–13.

We finished the season in Hawaii. Once again, our defense killed us, and the Rainbow Warriors hung 42 points on us. Fortunately, we came away 48–42 winners. Wins are rarely disappointing, but that one didn't exactly put a bounce in our step.

That left us at 9–3 on the season, prompting a lot of people to grumble when we accepted a bid to play the University of Florida in the Sugar Bowl. We knew there would be some changes going into the bowl game, as Gary Darnell had been offered a coaching position on John Mackovic's staff at the University of Texas. Coach Holtz had an unwritten rule: if you got a coaching job elsewhere, you left the staff immediately. Conducting business that way made for fewer distractions for both programs. Thus, Gary left Notre Dame prior to the bowl game, prompting Coach Holtz to move me to coach the inside linebackers against the explosive Gators offense, masterminded by Steve Spurrier.

Quarterback Shane Matthews led the No. 3 Gators' potent offense. He'd earned Southeastern Conference Player of the Year honors, and the Gators had posted a 10–1 record in Spurrier's second season as the head coach at his alma mater.

I'd been on the LSU sidelines the year before, when we lost, 34–8, to the Gators, so I'd seen firsthand what type of potent attack "The Ole Ball Coach" had put together in Gainesville.

It was for the level of competition and a number of other reasons that I looked forward to that Sugar Bowl. Being in New Orleans would put me back around many of the friends I'd left seven months earlier. My parents attended the game, which gave Dad a chance to spend time with his two youngest brothers, Bill and David, who lived and worked in New Orleans. Plus, it afforded me the opportunity to spend time with Mary Gayle, who could be a part of the Bowl festivities and spend more time with my parents and some of the coaches' wives.

Dad realized I was getting serious with Mary Gayle. I could tell that he really liked being around her. The giveaway came in how he started to tease me and jab at me about her like only he could. He definitely approved.

Once we arrived in New Orleans, Coach Holtz went out to dinner, where a waiter told him that the Sugar Bowl between the Fighting Irish and the Gators had come to be known as "The Cheerios Bowl." He explained that "The difference between Cheerios and Notre Dame is that Cheerios belong in a bowl."

Coach Holtz didn't care for the comment even though the waiter had just delivered motivational gold. The motivator in Coach Holtz used the waiter's slight accordingly.

As if we needed further motivation, we wore our white jerseys with green lettering that the players really liked.

Florida moved the ball up and down the field all night. Matthews threw for 511 yards, but when they got into the red zone, we would show four down linemen, but we would drop two and rush two. That threw their timing off and clogged the passing lanes on the shortened field. Seven times they were in the red zone, yet they only scored two touchdowns.

We trailed, 16–7, at the half. That's when Coach Holtz challenged the offensive line—who outweighed the Gators by thirty-five pounds a man—to take care of business. He felt as though they could lead the way to a victory, and they proved him correct. We committed to running the ball and keeping the defense off the field. Meanwhile, Jerome Bettis put on display what a force he could be. "The Bus" had incredible athleticism, particularly for someone who weighed 250 pounds. He's easily the best running back I'd ever been around, and none of my defensive guys ever wanted to tackle him during practices. The Gators didn't look too thrilled to try and bring him down either as he scored on touchdown runs of three and forty-nine yards to stake us to a 32–22 lead.

Florida responded with a thirty-six-yard scoring strike from Matthews to Harrison Houston with 2:28 left to make it 32–28. But we put the game out of reach on the following possession, when Bettis ran one in from thirty-nine yards out, making the final score 39–28.

Ultimately, our offense finished with just 279 total yards—paltry compared to the Gators' totals, and 141 of those yards came in the fourth quarter. Bettis finished the game with 150 yards rushing and in turn led us to victory.

During the press conference following the game, Coach Holtz

enjoyed the last laugh, not with just the win, but his rebuttal to the waiter, when he responded with his own question: "Do you know the difference between a golf pro and Lou Holtz?" Answer: "Lou Holtz doesn't give tips!"

Coach Holtz could certainly be funny, but when it came to business, he was sincere. As he told me in the locker room after the game, "Don't you talk to anybody. You're not going anywhere. You've got a job here. Don't talk to anybody."

I didn't, so I became a paid member of Coach Holtz's staff, coaching the outside linebackers and special teams.

Once we capped the '91 season with that great Sugar Bowl win over the Gators, I had more time to focus on my personal life.

The opportunity to spend a couple weeks in Louisiana with Mary Gayle encouraged me to think about making our relationship a permanent one. We began talking about the future and what that would look like for us. The next thing I knew, April had rolled around, and we had begun to plan a summer wedding in Baton Rouge and build a new house in Granger, Indiana—yet I still had not formally proposed to her!

In fact, as the house began to rise out of the ground, and wedding plans were being made, Mary Gayle reminded me of that fact one night while we talked on the phone. She had begun to feel uneasy about our situation. All these plans were going on, and she had no ring and no formal proposal. I am sure her friends were wondering what kind of guy planned a wedding and built a house without a ring and asking for her hand in marriage. I diverted the subject that night and told her not to worry. You see, I had a plan, but it couldn't be executed until June.

Back in February, when I made a weekend visit to Baton Rouge, we had gone shopping, and Mary Gayle had expressed that she really liked a ring at Barker's Antique Jewelry. I played it cool and said let's keep looking. Little did she know I had the owner send the ring to me. I knew I'd be speaking at a coaches' clinic in Los Angeles in June, and I wanted her to join me in California, so I could formally ask her to marry me while out there. Nothing like the last minute!

Dad's influence of music and theater had been so ingrained in me that even my proposal had his fingerprints all over it. After my clinic, I had hotel reservations to stay at the Ritz Carlton in Marina Del Rey, which Artie Gigantino, the defensive coordinator at USC, helped me arrange. I rented a limousine with a dozen roses and champagne to take us to the site where many Academy Awards had taken place, the Music Center of Los Angeles County. I'd thought of everything—a play, dinner, and a drive on Malibu Beach. What more could you ask for? My favorite play and soundtrack, *Phantom of the Opera*, played at the music center that weekend. But like many plans that are made, you sometimes have to call an audible. Turned out the limousine went to the wrong Ritz. The hotel told us to use their limo and I would just meet the other limo at the theater at the end of the play. Eventually, we made it to the play with little time to spare.

Just before intermission, there is a point where the boyfriend, Raoul, is singing a song to Christine titled "All I Ask of You." I had heard and sung this song hundreds of times, many of them with Dad. I even sang it at the wedding of Todd Caplin, my best man, several years prior. Raoul sings to Christine, asking her to share one lifetime. He will lead her away from her loneliness and will never leave her side. Wherever she travels, he will always be with her, and above all, he wants her to just "love him!"

That served as my cue to take Mary Gayle's hand. I slipped the ring on her finger and asked, "Will you?"

Thank God through her tears she smiled and said yes.

Shortly after getting the desired response, I left her before the intermission concluded so I could find out where our limo driver had parked. When I returned, I couldn't find her, and the bell to alert everyone to get back to their seats had begun to ring. Still, no Mary Gayle.

Finally, a little Spanish-speaking woman walked up to me and asked in broken English, "You looking for pretty blonde lady?"

I told her yes.

She escorted me to a closet door. My future bride sat in a broom closet with several teary-eyed women doting over her and helping her put scotch tape around the ring to make it tighter. The ring was to big and had not been correctly sized yet.

After the show, we found our limo driver with the dozen roses and champagne on ice. I don't think I could have planned any better on how it all came together. Yes, sometimes audibles do score touchdowns!

After a sixteen-month courtship, Mary Gayle and I were married.

Funny thing about the wedding planning is that it wasn't just as simple as abiding by our two schedules. As it turned out, during my first season at Notre Dame, I had become good friends with Coach Holtz's son, Skip, and our lives would be forever intertwined. We played a lot of golf together, worked out together, and one thing we both enjoyed was our late afternoon or evening spins around the Notre Dame campus on our rollerblades. Even our dating lives were in tandem. We both had been dating girls who lived hundreds of miles away, and, ultimately, we had to plan our weddings around each other's.

After spring recruiting and summer camps, the coaching staff only got three weeks of vacation in July. Thus, I took the first week for our wedding, July 3, and Skip took the second week, July 11. We were groomsmen for each other, so that led to a lot of planning. The third week would be our honeymoon time. Mary Gayle and I were off to Barbados, and Skip and Jennifer were off to the Cayman Islands, until one day in April, Skip walked into my office and asked me, "Do you mind if we go to Barbados with you all?" His trip had been canceled, so I said, "Sure, but we have to agree that we won't see each other for at least three of the days. You know what I mean?" (Wink-wink) I'll always remember that summer for being a magical time in my life. Sharing that time with lifelong friends only enhanced the experience.

Everything in my life seemed to be clicking into place, on the personal front as well as the professional one.

The 1992 season proved to be a success even though we fell short of our ultimate goal to win a National Championship. We survived the Michigan game in South Bend the second week of the season, and our only loss that year came to Stanford, 33–16, in the first week of October.

It was certainly a plus that that 1992 team had so many seniors and future NFL players, like Rick Mirer, Jerome Bettis, Demetrius Dubose, Tom Carter, Craig Hentrich, Irv Smith, and Devon McDonald. Ultimately, we played Texas A&M in the 1993 Cotton Bowl and beat them handily, 28–3, to finish strong and earn a No. 4 ranking in the UPI and AP polls at the end of the year.

I sent Dad a card in November to thank him for all he had done to help me find my way:

Dear Dad,

I have been going through a lot of soul-searching the past few months. Looking back at my past, how I have attained the present and where I will be in the future. God has watched over me but mostly, my father has watched over me. He kept the firm hand on me when I needed it and he gave me more rope when he thought I could use it. I know I could not be where I am today without your help and support, and it is only right that my business cards say "Joe Wessel" because part of you is up here with me. Every time I walk out on the field, part of Joe Sr. is walking out there with

Joe Jr. I hope I have made you proud and I hope you strut your feathers a little bit because there are very few fathers that can say, "My boy coaches at Notre Dame." . . . I love you Dad, and in all the business and running around I do, if I haven't told you that, thanks and remember that you are appreciated more than one can say!

All my love, Tiger

CHAPTER 17

Coping and Overcoming

MARY GAYLE GAVE ME A small, wrapped package on Christmas Day, 1992. When I unwrapped the box, I experienced one of the most euphoric feelings of my life. Inside, I found an antique silver baby rattle wrapped in a blue ribbon. She was pregnant, and with a boy. There were twenty-one grandchildren from Esther and Louis, yet this baby would be the first to carry the Wessel name! The pregnancy brought an exciting time. My body wasn't transforming like my wife's, but I stood by her side cheering her every move and coaching her on during a bitter cold winter in South Bend complete with plenty of snow.

I'd long heard that women get cravings during the pregnancy. True to form, the craving in our household was watermelon. I did my best to help her satisfy that craving, but watermelon wasn't exactly the easiest item to find in South Bend grocery stores (remember, South Bend is the snow belt of the Midwest). Nevertheless, we got through that winter and spring, and all was well when we reached the summer months.

Despite the fact that I was about to be a parent myself, I still took quite seriously the advice and support offered by Dad and, of course, Mom, too. I wrote the following to my mother in a letter dated August 3, 1993:

Dear Mom,

. . . Things are just fine up here. Mary Gayle is doing super, but she is getting very uncomfortable at night. I hope you can work out your schedule to be with her when she has the baby. I want you to know that she wants so much for you to be there for her. She is very apprehensive and all she has is you as a mother-in-law, Margie and Ann Marie [my sisters]. She wants to be able to share this experience with "family." Unfortunately, "we" are her only family.

She depends on me and all of you for that support. You and Dad have been super keeping in contact with us. . . . The past few months have really shown me how important life is. My marriage and this baby are almost larger than life itself.

No "job" or "win" can make me feel more content than the way I feel for my wife and soon-to-be child. There are many ingredients to make a "happy and healthy relationship." I feel that the love and closeness of Mary Gayle and my family must be the most important thing there is right now. She wants it, I want it, I hope everyone down there wants it. I also hope that everyone will be conscious of the fact that she needs you all!

To be honest, I also need you all!

All my love

Mom and Dad reacted like they always did, with 100 percent support, and they planned to be in South Bend the day we came home from the hospital.

In the meantime, fall practice was approaching, and based on all the quality seniors we'd lost from the previous season, expectations were not so lofty entering the 1993 season. Still, at Notre Dame, you were always expected to be challenging for the National Championship. That year, I coached the defensive backs, and they were arguably one of the best group of defensive backs to play at Notre Dame.

Luck was on my side that season. I had a veteran group returning that consisted of three starters and three others who contributed greatly to our success. All of them were later drafted and made NFL teams—Jeff Burris, Bobby Taylor, John Covington, Sean Wooden, Willie Clark, and Greg Lane.

We beat Northwestern at home in the opener, and in week two, we traveled to the "Big House" ranked No. 11 in the polls to play No. 3 Michigan. We beat the Wolverines, 27–23, on September 11, which happened to be the 400th game played at the University of Michigan. Following that win, we bused back to South Bend and began preparation for Michigan State.

The week after the Michigan game coincided with an important event. On Monday, September 13, 1993, we went to the hospital, where the doctor was scheduled to induce labor. We were so excited. The long-awaited time had arrived. We would soon be meeting our son. Running down the stairs that morning, I remember pausing and saying to myself, *Ugh, today is the 13th; I'm just glad it's not a Friday.*

When we arrived at the hospital, we were escorted into the last room down the hall in the maternity ward, and the process began. By midday, the excitement started to build. I had played and coached in huge stadiums in front of large crowds, yet I'd never been as nervous as I found myself that afternoon. Around 2 o'clock, the doctor entered the room to check one of the monitors. They had lost the baby's heartbeat, which happens from time to time. The next thing I knew, three other people were in the room desperately racing around in chaos. If that weren't enough, the doctor's face showed shock and disbelief. They kept trying to find a heartbeat with internal monitors, but to no avail. After fifteen or twenty minutes, the attending doctor said, "We lost him!"

I'm thinking, *What do you mean we lost him? How could this be?*

We trusted you to deliver our baby! God wouldn't let this happen! I was a coach and husband. Protecting my family and solving problems and issues were a part of what I did. I felt helpless. I had no idea what to say or do. My emotional high earlier had turned into the worst day of my life. The hurt and loss from that day has remained with me since.

Despite all of the emotions running through me, I had no time for self-pity. Helping Mary Gayle deal with the emotional and physical pain she felt became my priority. I needed and wanted to comfort her. She had carried this baby for nine months. And now we wouldn't be bringing him home. All I could do was to lie next to her, cry with her, and hold her. Our lives were forever changed. The pain of 1979, losing my best friend, was resurrected within me. Only this felt ten times worse, and so much more personal.

The doctors came back in and told us what they thought happened. They thought vasa praevia had caused the unthinkable outcome. They said they would not know for sure until after the baby was delivered. They recommended that we continue the process naturally so there would not be unnecessary surgery. So early the next morning, we gave birth to "Baby Wessel" knowing we would not hear the cry that we longed for over the past nine months. We went home empty-handed, full of sorrow, anger, disbelief, and doubt whether we would ever have this chance again. In times like these, you don't know what to say to others, and they certainly don't know what to say to you. I called the football office that afternoon and told my secretary what had happened. Father Paul Doyle, who married us and was a Notre Dame alum and rector of Corby Hall at the time, came to the hospital. He prayed with me and tried to give me comfort, but he could not give words to explain why this had happened.

Mary Gayle remained in the hospital for a couple days, and my parents flew up to help in the interim. One night when my father and I came back from the hospital, we sat in the car in the garage listening to a song from the play *Les Misérables*, "Bring him Home."

We had listened to this song hundreds of times in the past. Now the lyrics had a whole different meaning for us. Valjean in the play is praying to God to protect Marius, his soon-to-be son-in-law. He asks God to protect him and bring him home safely. While sitting there with tears flowing from my eyes, I knew that God now had another angel with him in heaven. I told Dad I wanted to sing this song at his funeral. I still don't know why I told Dad that. Probably because I knew he'd understand without pushing for further explanation.

When tragedies affect our lives, we tend to feel isolated and despondent. In the days following our loss, we had many people share their stories and their pain, including several colleagues at Notre Dame. I found everyone's stories comforting. One particular colleague whose support I valued was basketball coach John MacLeod. His office was two doors down, and he made it a point to pop into my office daily. His words of encouragement were exactly what Dad would have told me had I been in Florida.

Throughout the following weeks, Dad was not physically with me, but his phone calls and letters kept encouraging me to remain strong in my faith and to trust in God's plan. He urged me to be patient with myself and, more important, to be patient with Mary Gayle. He knew I was hurting, but he reinforced that my love and care for her was critical during this period of time. You either grow apart or you grow together experiencing what we did. Over time, we would heal, and we did so together, growing even closer.

Getting back to practice brought me a much-needed distraction. The players and coaches were so thoughtful. My veteran group of defensive backs didn't miss a beat. We beat Michigan State, 36–14, that week. We then won six more to set up that season's "Game of the Century" with No. 1 Florida State. We were ranked No. 2, and my alma mater would be traveling to South Bend for what would turn out to be a memorable game on November 13, Mom's birthday.

So much hoopla and buildup took place prior to the "Game of the Century" that pitted unbeaten teams at the top of the rankings against each other, a rare spectacle that doesn't happen very often in college football: No. 1 vs. No. 2!

FSU was stacked with standouts and future NFL players, with 1993 Heisman Trophy winner Charlie Ward headlining the crew.

Personally, the week leading up to that game proved to be very distracting for me, between the guests coming into town and the media from all over looking for unique stories to the game like the one about us losing our child.

In typical fashion around a high-profile game, journalists sought out new story angles. Gary Long, who covered college football for the *Miami Herald*, wrote a story about our loss. The headline for that November 12, 1993, article read: "Tragedy trivializes Irish-FSU showdown."

In the article, I was quoted talking about our loss as follows: "This game's outcome is so trivial when you think about things like [a child's death]."

I told Long: "God has a plan for us all. You have to believe in that plan, whether or not you can agree with it or understand it."

In addition, the many connections that existed between Notre Dame and FSU kept everyone very busy, catching up with old friends and colleagues (though, interestingly, the two schools had only played once before—in 1981, which had been my redshirt year—and FSU won, 19–13). Coach Holtz was very friendly with Coach Bowden. They used to vacation together on summer trips. Skip Holtz had been a grad assistant for Coach Bowden in the late '80s. Mickey Andrews was still the defensive coordinator, and several other FSU coaches were still there from when I played. Two of the coaches, Jeff Bowden and Odell Hagans, played with me during my days at Florida State.

As part of the additional excitement leading up to this special game, Notre Dame had a tradition of holding a pep rally in the basketball arena the night before every home football game. At each pep rally, one or two assistant coaches were assigned by Coach Holtz to speak, and, of course, I had been picked to speak prior to the Florida State game.

I thought long and hard about what I could do or say to get Notre Dame fans pumped up while not disparaging my alma mater. I decided I needed a prop. FSU arrived in town wearing green baseball caps that were embroidered with the FSU logo in gold lettering, so I asked our equipment man to get me two Seminoles spear decals and put them on one of our Notre Dame helmets. The end product resembled an FSU helmet, only shinier. When I wrapped up my speech, I pulled out the helmet from underneath the podium. The boos became deafening. I calmed the Notre Dame faithful once I began to rip the decals off each side of the helmet. I told them, "Under every great team . . . there lies a golden dome!"

Well, that brought the place to a frenzy, and it was a big hit, though it wasn't appreciated by my sister, mother, and FSU friends. Of course, Dad, a Miami Hurricane, absolutely loved it.

Notre Dame dominated the game, but FSU scored with 1:39 left in the fourth quarter. On a fourth-and-20, Brian Magee deflected a Charlie Ward pass, and Kez McCorvey hauled in the ball for a touchdown that cut our lead to 31–24.

FSU kicked off to us, then managed to get the ball back within three plays. Once again, the magical Ward moved the 'Noles down the field to our 14-yard line. But with three seconds left to play, Shawn Wooden knocked down a pass in the end zone to save the win for Notre Dame.

After that, I just broke down. All the heartache of the past two months had built up, and I was emotionally exhausted. I rode the elevator down from the press box with Mark Richt, the FSU offensive coordinator, who I played against when he was at Miami; and Brad Scott, who had been a grad assistant when I played at FSU. I told them they did a great job and wished them luck the rest of the way.

My trip back to the locker room took me past the FSU bench. Sitting on the bench were two green hats that had been discarded.

By the end of the season, the bowl outlook shaped up for a No. 1 Notre Dame vs. No. 2 FSU rematch in the Fiesta Bowl on New Year's Day. Unfortunately, that matchup got derailed the following week when we lost, 41–39, to a Boston College team coached by Tom Coughlin. He'd go on to win a couple of Super Bowls as the head coach of the New York Giants.

Boston College kicked a 41-yard field goal as time expired to ruin our undefeated season. We dropped to No. 4 in the rankings, granting us an invitation to play Texas A&M in the Cotton Bowl for a second consecutive year.

In the weeks prior to the bowl game, Rick Minter, our defensive coordinator, was hired as the head coach at the University of Cincinnati. Pursuant to Coach Holtz's policy regarding coaches who had accepted other jobs, Minter departed, paving the way for me to be promoted to defensive coordinator for the Cotton Bowl.

We played well on New Year's Day of 1994 and beat the Aggies, 24–21. Florida State squeaked out a win against Nebraska in the Orange Bowl later that night. We all watched that game in the hotel, and we felt we'd share the National Championship with FSU. What more could I ask for, having cochampions between the school I worked for and the school where I'd played college football?

The following day, the Associated Press Poll and the United Press International Poll declared FSU No. 1 and Notre Dame No. 2. Coach Bowden finally won that elusive first National Championship. While I felt happy for him, I felt like we'd been shortchanged at Notre Dame. After all, we had beat FSU head-to-head.

The 1993 season should have been one of the best six months of my life. Although there were eleven wins on the field, the one loss off the field would never be forgotten and will be etched in my heart forever.

CHAPTER 18

On to the NFL

BEING AT NOTRE DAME AND coaching under Coach Holtz probably shaped me more as a coach and as a person than I had experienced in my life. Expectations at Notre Dame were off the charts, as were Coach Holtz's.

Everyone who arrives at Notre Dame expects a National Championship. Coaches, players, staff, trainers, professors, administrators, and even the student body expected the Irish to be in the top spot once the season finished. Coach Holtz reminded you of that fact every single day. The roller coaster of emotions in a football season brings the best and the worst out in all of us. I had my share of life's emotions during my three years at South Bend.

Coach Holtz knew how to motivate his players, a real master. His words, his preparation, his organizational skills, and his ability to push people past their tipping points made him unique. He ran the football organization like a hands-on CEO, challenging everybody all the time. At times, it might have seemed way too much, but many times it brought what the situation needed.

Coach Holtz held his players accountable, and he held his coaches even more accountable. It was something I'd always admired and replicated later in my life.

Following the 1993 season, I wanted to become the defensive coordinator at Notre Dame. I felt like a strong candidate, too; after all, I'd been the interim defensive coordinator during the Cotton Bowl. In addition, during my time at LSU, I didn't have the defensive coordinator title, but I called every defense because I was the only coach who understood how to tie the defensive front to the secondary. Of course, when I got to Notre Dame, the same thing happened a couple of times. I knew I could do the job.

Two days after we returned to South Bend from our Cotton Bowl win, Coach Holtz and the staff took off for the coaches' convention in Anaheim. When I got to the hotel, everybody I saw told me, "Hey, Coach Holtz is looking for you. He wants to interview you."

Interview me?

I went to his room and knocked on his door. When he answered, he told me he wanted to schedule some time with me that week to interview me for the open defensive coordinator position. Coach Holtz wanted it to be a fair process.

Instead, I countered, "Why don't we do it now?"

"You sure?" he asked.

I nodded. "Coach, you know me. You know what you're getting with me. Let's do it right now."

Coach Holtz shrugged. "Okay, come on in."

He only asked me two questions. After the second, he told me, "That's good enough."

At the time, I couldn't understand why the interview had been so brief. Later, I realized he'd probably simply been checking the box that said he'd interviewed me.

A week or so after returning to South Bend from the coaching conference, I go to my desk and see a 5 x 7 card that read: "Joe, Bob Davie has accepted the defensive coordinator's job at the University of Notre Dame!—Coach Holtz."

That's how he told me I didn't get the job. I loved Notre Dame and I could have been happy staying there forever, but after that, I recognized the time had come for me to move on. I've never talked to Coach Holtz about why he chose Davie over me.

Coach Holtz knew I planned on leaving. That's one of those sensitive areas where you usually don't tell the head coach you're leaving, but I needed his help when David Shula came calling.

My decision to leave Notre Dame was twofold—it had to do with my disappointment at not getting the defensive coordinator position, and the other part came down to getting a chance to coach at the NFL level. While every college coach can say he loves college, if somebody walked in and gave him an NFL contract, nine out of ten would take it.

Guilty as charged.

When old friend David Shula became the head coach of the Cincinnati Bengals in 1992 at age thirty-two, he became one of the youngest head coaches in the history of the NFL. After the 1993 season, he offered me a job on his staff coaching the defensive line. Larry Peccatiello had just gotten the job as the Bengals' defensive coordinator, and he and Coach Holtz had coached together at William & Mary back in the 1960s.

Shula offered me the defensive line coaching job. I'd never coached that position before, but I assured him I could do it. I felt comfortable knowing the outside of the defensive end structure, and I knew I could learn the inside. I liked the experience the job would give me, since I'd already coached the defensive backs and linebackers. If I went to interview for another defensive coordinator position, I would have coached all the defensive positions. From a résumé standpoint, that would be huge.

Still, moving to the NFL brought some challenges. Naturally, I consulted with Dad about the opportunity. Typical of my father's blunt speaking, he first asked if I knew what I was doing. I'd shared a lot with him over the previous nine years. When I told him I felt confident in what I was doing, he endorsed the move. He always trusted my judgment when making some of my biggest decisions.

Most assumed the money drove my decision. I did make a little more money—I made $56,000 at Notre Dame and $75,000 at Cincinnati. But the move really wasn't a question of money. I wanted to have an opportunity to coach in the biggest arena, and I trusted David Shula with my life.

Coach Holtz decided to leave the Notre Dame job in 1996 without offering much of a reason.

Davie served as the Notre Dame head coach until getting fired after five years in the position. To this day, I still wonder to where I could have ascended had Coach Holtz made me the defensive coordinator. Dad and I spoke about this, but he rarely played the "what if" game.

Coaching in the NFL differed from coaching in college in many ways. In the NFL, if you didn't think a player fit into your plan, you could get rid of him and go get someone else. Sometimes ownership would get rid of someone even if you thought that he would be a productive player.

Even though the Bengals had appeared in two Super Bowls, losing to the San Francisco 49ers in both, they had a unique organization. Mike Brown and his family ran the show.

Initially, I felt anxious when I began to work at my new job. Lucky for me, I had an experienced group on the defensive line, and they were very helpful. Tim Krumrie led that group. An eleven-year veteran, Krumrie had been an All-Pro selection and had played in the 1988 Super Bowl. The experience he brought to the defensive line helped me a lot.

Since I'd coached the outside linebackers my first two years at Notre Dame, I had some perspective on the defensive line. I had one guy who rushed and one who played coverage. I studied a lot of film and talked and visited with several people. Tom Pratt, the Kansas City Chiefs defensive line coach, helped me a lot. I met him on a plane during a scouting trip. He'd played college ball at the University of Miami, and we just hit it off. Joe Greene helped me out a lot, too. "Mean Joe" had a Hall of Fame career playing for the Pittsburgh Steelers during their "Steel Curtain" defense's heyday. Greene coached with the Dolphins at the time, so we had a connection.

That first season with the Bengals, I had Alfred Williams on my defensive line. He'd been a first-round pick out of the University of Colorado in 1991. Prior to the 1994 season, he wanted the Bengals to pay him more money or to trade him. That stance prompted him to become a holdout. I didn't meet him until the first day of training camp. During that initial meeting, he went off on a tirade laced with F-bombs about how the Bengals ownership had screwed him. Once I got him calmed down, I promised him that if he did what I asked him to do, I'd help him get out of Cincinnati. Two weeks later, Mary Gayle and I were having dinner in an Outback Steakhouse in Cincinnati, when the waitress brought over a bottle of wine to our table. She told us a guy from across the room had sent the bottle our way, then she pointed out Alfred, along with Kanavis McGhee, another defensive end on the team. "Big Al" came over and apologized for his tirade and explained it wasn't meant to be personal to me. I always remembered that and thought highly of him to do that.

By the time I coached with the Bengals, Dad's singing performances had tapered off. He did sing with the Florida Philharmonic Orchestra and Chorus, and he performed for the Miami Opera Guild. Many times, Dad's performances bordered on the operatic because throughout his life he'd been a stickler to old Latin in the Catholic church. He loved Italian opera. Luciano Pavarotti ranked as one of his favorites. Otherwise, Dad pretty much limited his performances to choirs, weddings, and funerals. He still had the talent, but being the perfectionist he was, I don't think he felt comfortable with the sound he produced. However, he did perform "The Star-Spangled Banner" at Cincinnati's Cinergy Field prior to the Bengals-New Orleans Saints game on September 15, 1996. I had heard they were looking for someone to sing, and I volunteered Dad.

I'd seen Dad perform before, but never the National Anthem. Standing on the sidelines while he sang gave me goose bumps, and I teared up while he delivered a flawless performance. That definitely ranked as a highlight from my days coaching with the Bengals.

While in Cincinnati, I played a lot of golf with Bruce Coslet, the offensive coordinator, and Kenny Anderson, the quarterback coach and former Bengals great. Dick LeBeau, Hall of Fame defensive back and defensive coordinator for the Steelers, joined us many times on the golf course.

I guess the fact that I played a lot of golf made me think of Dad and ways we could enjoy the game together. After all, he had taught me the game. Having the Nicklaus connection, some wild ideas began to percolate. I'm not sure if it was the confidence attained now that I was an NFL coach, but it was around this time that I started to think big. Still in touch with Steve and Jack Nicklaus, I wondered what Jack might say if I approached him about a golf outing at Augusta National.

So it was that I reached out to Jack by writing him a letter. Dad regularly traveled to play golf all over the world, so I asked Jack, if ever an opportunity presented itself where I could get Dad up to Augusta to play golf, whether he could help us make that happen. In response, I received a pleasant letter from Jack. He said he couldn't accommodate my request. Of course, I understood he probably got fifty such requests a month. I appreciated him being open with me.

However, I had bigger frustrations to attend to, on the professional front. The Bengals had the top pick in the 1994 draft and selected nose guard Dan Wilkinson from Ohio State. My frustrations stemmed from the fact I felt as though Notre Dame's Bryant Young would be a better player and had a bigger motor. During a predraft meeting, I expressed that opinion when asked which of the two I would take. They thought I had a bias to my opinion since I'd coached at Notre Dame. That might have been true, but ultimately Young played fourteen years for the San Francisco 49ers and made the Pro Bowl four times. He finished with 89.5 career sacks, ranking him at fourth all-time in the NFL in career sacks for defensive tackles, trailing only Trevor Pryce and Hall of Famers John Randle and Warren Sapp. Bryant also ranks third on the 49ers' all-time career sacks list, placing him behind defensive ends Tommy Hart and Cedric Hardman, and owns the 49ers' franchise record for career safeties, with three. Ultimately, he became a member of the NFL's All-Decade Team of the 1990s. Meanwhile, Wilkinson played for four teams during a thirteen-year career that never lived up to expectations. In fairness to Wilkinson, expectations for him were extremely high.

Another draft story that didn't exactly turn out well for the Bengals occurred the next year when we had the fifth overall pick. Heading into the big day, our plan had been to use our first pick to select University of Florida defensive end Kevin Carter. Then we planned to come back and use our second-round pick, the thirty-sixth pick of the draft, on University of Pittsburgh running back Curtis Martin. Instead, we traded our picks to the Carolina Panthers, who had the number-one pick, so we could select Penn State running back Ki-Jana Carter.

Sadly, Ki-Jana Carter's NFL career never really happened. After tearing his ACL in a preseason game, he missed his rookie season. The next season, he returned to gain 2.9 yards per carry on 91 yards. In eight NFL seasons, Ki-Jana gained 1,144 yards and scored eight touchdowns.

Conversely, the St. Louis Rams drafted Kevin Carter with the sixth pick of the draft, meaning, in theory, he still would have been on the board when we selected with the fifth pick of the draft. Since the New England Patriots selected Martin with the seventy-fourth pick of the draft, he too would have been available had we just remained pat and stuck to our original draft plan.

Martin, of course, had a Hall of Fame career, and Kevin Carter compiled 104.5 sacks during fourteen NFL seasons.

On the positive side, David had a great rapport with the players. That didn't come as a shock, since a lot of them were right around his age. He always remained positive and energetic—the eternal optimist—throughout his stint. Clearly, he had his mother's remarkable outlook.

Under David, the Bengals went 8–24 in the two seasons before I arrived. We went 3–13 in 1994. After one season as the defensive line coach—a position I'd never coached—I became the special-teams coach prior to the 1995 season.

That 1995 season proved to be better than the previous season's outcome. We won our first two games but lost the next four. The rest of the season felt like a yo-yo—win one, then lose one. Win one, then lose one. We couldn't sustain putting back-to-back wins together and finished 7–9. Even though we'd finished with a losing record, Bengals fans had cause for hope heading into the 1996 season.

Away from the field, Mary Gayle and I got some good news. After three years of dealing with the loss of our baby and hoping, praying, and making plenty of visits to the doctor, we received the news we were expecting a son in September of 1996.

Having experienced heartbreak in the past, I couldn't help but be skeptical, nervous, and anxious about what the future would bring. That had to be the longest nine months of my life. Every doctor visit came chock full of trepidation and anxiety. I wanted to be positive, but the loss lingered in the back of my head. My heart remained broken. Through it all, we never lost hope.

In mid-August, we agreed with the doctors to schedule an induced labor on September 3. That fell on the Tuesday prior to our second game of the season, against the Chargers in San Diego. Having the baby delivered on that day gave me more flexibility, because that was the players' day off with no practice.

We'd lost the opener, 26–16, to the Rams in St. Louis. Since we lost that one, we knew we had to have good game plan prepared for the Chargers. I did my best to keep my focus while my thoughts and emotions were all about getting through the next two days and bringing home my son.

My parents had come up to Cincinnati to help. Getting baby and Mom home presented a lot of logistical problems, and having them there to help address some of those certainly helped. However, their presence came mostly in the way of moral support.

Dad had a flight from Cincinnati to San Diego on that Thursday for the game. He would be staying with Jerry Sullivan, who coached the Chargers wide receivers. Dad got to know Jerry when we coached together at LSU, having attended dinner one night with me, Jerry, and John Mitchell, our defensive line coach. Jerry, having been born and raised in Miami, had a lot to talk about with Dad that night.

Finally, the big day arrived. On September 3, 1996, Mary Gayle, Mom, Dad, and I woke up early. At 11 a.m., we were introduced to a healthy baby boy we named Louis Trenton Hamilton Wessel—"Trent" for short.

Being there and watching the birth of a child is the most over-whelming feeling a human can ever experience. As the doctor gave me the scissors to cut the umbilical cord, I stood there in awe of God's creation. To this day, thinking about it brings a smile to my face and tears to my eyes. After all the doctor appointments, along with the pain and anxiety we endured over the previous three years, we were finally bringing home a long-awaited, and cherished, gift.

I spent several hours getting Mary Gayle and Trent settled in the hospital, before I had to leave. The Chargers were our next opponent, and they didn't care that I had had a new son. I had to get back to work to help put a game plan together for Sunday.

We lost to the Chargers, 27–14, before returning home and breaking into the win column with a 30–15 win against the New Orleans Saints. We then dropped three consecutive games to fall to 1–5 on the season.

We traveled to San Francisco to face the 49ers in our seventh game. Playing at 3Com Park—formerly known as Candlestick Park—we built a 21–0 second-quarter lead before the 49ers got busy. They ran off 28 unanswered points. Future Hall of Fame quarterback Steve Young ran one in from fifteen yards for the final score in our 28–21 defeat.

David got fired the following day.

That move stunned all of us.

David called and told me what had happened. He took the news hard, obviously. He's an emotional guy. And getting fired from a job you love is a tough deal.

David left coaching and became the president of Shula's Steakhouse, and in 2018, he returned to the coaching ranks at his alma mater, Dartmouth, coaching the wide receivers.

Bruce Coslet, our offensive coordinator, got named the interim head coach. Even though I felt bad for David, I didn't think I'd have any trouble keeping my job. Bruce and I were more than just coaching acquaintances and golfing buddies; I felt we were friends. Mary Gayle even did some design work in his home.

We won three consecutive games after Bruce took over as the head coach, and four of our final six games, to finish at 8–8. That strong end to the season prompted the powers that be to take away Bruce's interim title and make him the head coach.

Bruce told me after that season that he could only promise me a defensive assistant's job, which was like a graduate assistant's job. He added: "There are nine openings out there I know about. If I were you, I'd go ahead and see if you can find something that will guarantee you as a full-time assistant job." He couldn't tell me who he planned on hiring to be his defensive coordinator. Whether or not I'd get hired by him for one of the defensive jobs—not a defensive assistant's job—would be up to the guy Bruce hired to be the defensive coordinator.

At that point, I had not put two and two together about who Bruce planned to hire to be his defensive coordinator. It was so obvious in hindsight, but when you're going through the emotions of fighting for your professional career, you become somewhat blind.

Yet football is a business. And so it was that after the season, I traveled with a Bengals contingent to the East-West Shrine Game in California. Afterward, we went to the Senior Bowl in Alabama. That's when Bruce dropped a bombshell on me.

We were standing around on the field in the middle of the first day of practice, when Bruce sidled up to me.

He had decided to pull my offer to remain with the Bengals. Something went off inside of me, and I ripped into him. I had enough anger running through me at that point that I almost punched him. He didn't tell me why he pulled the offer, and to this day, I don't know why he did so. I have not spoken to Bruce since.

That left me having to hunt for a job once again. In the meantime, I found out that Bruce hired Dick LeBeau to be the defensive coordinator. Of course, that hiring drove me crazy, because I knew that Dick would have hired me to fill one of the defensive coaching positions.

Yet I couldn't change the decision, and the fact of the matter was

I had to find a job. Nolan Cromwell, the special-teams coach for the Packers, introduced me to Andy Reid, who was close with Ray Rhodes when they both were at Green Bay. He helped me get an interview with Rhodes, who was the Eagles head coach. In March, the Eagles hired me to be their special-teams coach.

That Eagles team had some coaching talent for sure. Jon Gruden served as the offensive coordinator, and Sean Payton coached the quarterbacks. Bill Callahan was the offensive line coach. They all became head coaches in the NFL.

Yet perhaps the most exciting part of being in Philly was the fact that it enabled me to add to my list of great golfing experiences with Dad.

I played golf at Heron Pines in New Jersey, and through that connection, I met and became friends with Bill McGuinness, an accomplished amateur golfer in the area who had played collegiate golf at Notre Dame.

Bill is a member at Pine Valley and Tavistock, and we shared many rounds together. That friendship opened the door for a great father-son golf trip when Bill connected me with a golfing friend of his, Dennis McCauley, who was a member at Winged Foot and Westchester. Dennis invited his father to round out our foursome. We played Pine Valley in Clementon, New Jersey, on a Thursday. From there, we headed north past New York City, landing at Westchester Country Club in the town of Harrison, New York, and thereafter also played Winged Foot Golf Club in Mamaroneck, New York. That trip also allowed us to visit the notorious Greenwich Village in New York City.

The Village had been the hub of the counterculture movement when Dad roamed those tree-lined streets as a young man. Off-Broadway theaters, restaurants, bars, and cafés were just as prevalent in Dad's heyday as they are today. Dad showed me the apartment building where he had lived while working toward becoming an entertainer. He'd also worked as a sous-chef and a chef. Being the oldest in a family of ten had taught him to cook. His mother had been a good cook, too, and everything was cooked from scratch back then. That proved to be a nostalgic trip for the both of us. I managed to get a sense of what his life had been like as a young, aspiring singer.

The downside of my time in Philadelphia came during a Monday Night Football game against the 49ers. Simply stated, their special teams beat our special teams, which made for a bad night for me personally. Particularly when that bad night occurred on national television during a Monday night telecast.

Since the day I got hired in Philadelphia, I had harped time and again that we needed some of our better players on the special teams. If you want to have quality special teams, you had to have quality players. Special teams are an important component of any team, and some coaches realized that fact more than others. Being on special teams is hazardous duty. Some coaches didn't want to run the risk of having one of their star players get his knee taken out while covering punts or kickoffs.

I didn't get the players I needed, and full protect mode was the rule in Philly. Special teams were treated almost like an afterthought. Boy, did that deficiency ever look glaring during the Monday night game.

At halftime of that game, the 49ers led, 24–6, even though their offense had the ball just eleven minutes and they made just six first downs. They ended up winning, 24–12, without scoring in the second half. According to others around the league, Dan Dierdorf beat me up with his commentary during the broadcast, which I did not see.

Philly fans had someone to blame.

Mike Lombardi, who served as a team consultant for the Eagles that year, told me, "Joe, now you know how Winston Churchill felt." I didn't understand, so I asked Mike, "What are you talking about?"

He explained that Winston Churchill cried for America to help England for two years, and when President Roosevelt visited England, the damage had already been done. That's exactly what happened to me. I compelled the power that be that we needed "teams" players. But by the time they starting bringing in players during the middle of the season, the buildings and bridges had already been blown up, along with my stay in Philadelphia.

I wasn't asked to return to Philadelphia for a second season.

John Harbaugh followed me as the Eagles special-teams coach, which I find ironic. Harbaugh, who is the current head coach of the Baltimore Ravens, had worked for Rick Minter at the University of Cincinnati. In 1994, Rick had asked me to help his rookie special-teams coach—Harbaugh—institute all the special-team units we used at Notre Dame. My struggles and John's influence must have given Philly's ownership a wake-up call to invest in players who could help the special teams.

Many years later, I saw John on the field during warm-ups before a Ravens-Bears game. John was very cordial and complimentary to me in front of my kids, who were with me. They thought he was so cool. We talked about the Eagles, Cincy, and his success at Baltimore. After twenty minutes, we shook hands, and I thanked him for spending that time with us. He walked away, then turned around and said, "Hey Joe, we special-teams guys have to stick together."

My experiences in Cincinnati and Philadelphia, along with the grind of trying to find the next coaching position, started to make me question the life I was leading as a football coach. I felt disenchanted with coaching. Having seen everything that I had gone through, Mary Gayle had grown disenchanted by my profession, as well.

I had a couple chances to stay in coaching at the college level, but I knew I would be chasing future opportunities to get back in the NFL. Effectively, my coaching career had run its course at that point.

God had a different plan for me, and I needed to start listening.

CHAPTER 19

Out of Coaching

At some time during every coaching stop I made, I'd sit around with the other coaches and we'd wonder what we would be doing if we weren't coaches. "What's the real world like?" we'd ask one another.

That conversation became reality for me after that disastrous 1997 season. I found myself struggling to stay in the league.

My contract with the Eagles was about to run out in March, I didn't have any offers to stay in coaching, and I had a wife and a young child. Talk about dancing on the edge of the volcano! I could feel the heat.

By March of 1998, I started to think, *What next?* I felt if I wanted to coach, I needed to have some enthusiasm and passion, but I was losing mine. Part of that could be attributed to always having to fight for a job and, more times than not, missing out on the opportunity—even when I felt like I was the most qualified candidate.

Two head coaches and two coordinators told me they could not interview me because I was white during a period when a big push was taking place to hire minorities in the NFL.

The Rooney Rule wasn't instituted in the NFL until the 2003 season. Once implemented, the rule required NFL teams to interview ethnic-minority candidates for head coaching and senior football operation jobs. Still, an initiative to get minorities into the coaching ranks had already begun. My wish for sports and all of society is that one day people are looked at for who they are and what they have accomplished and not because of their skin color or sex.

As a result of these hurdles, I decided to look for job opportunities outside of coaching.

When I talked to Dad about the prospect of leaving coaching, he didn't immediately jump on board to the idea. Instead, he did like he always did. He questioned me. He didn't want me to make an emotional decision and get out for the wrong reasons—just because I couldn't get a job. In the back of Dad's mind, he probably also thought about how he'd given up on his Broadway dream way too soon. Having that regret made him probe to try and find out whether I truly wanted to leave coaching. Surrendering a dream could lead to heartache, something he understood. On the other hand, he understood from our talks over the years about the grind of coaching and the toll that living a coach's life takes on your family life.

Ironically (or maybe not so ironically), both of my sisters had been coaches, as well. After Margie played volleyball at FSU, she became the head coach at Clemson for three years. My younger sister, Ann Marie, played volleyball at Clemson and went on to coach at Colorado State before becoming the head coach at Jacksonville University. Both subsequently left the profession.

When Don Shula first heard I planned on becoming a coach, he passed along the following wisdom: "The day you think you know it all is the day you should retire."

I thought about what Coach Shula told me while I pondered leaving the profession. I never felt like I knew everything about football. Retirement came my way anyway. Like Shula, my mother instilled in me at an early age the desire to be a life-long learner, which turned out to be a good thing, since I needed to find a new career outside of coaching.

Just when I really got busy looking for something else outside of coaching, God began to talk.

Jeff Fordham, who played with me at Fork Union and went on to play at LSU, lived in Atlanta and was best friends with an old Miami acquaintance, Pat Flood. I had played baseball and basketball against Pat in grammar school and high school. Jeff put me in contact with him. In addition to being CEO and president of HomeBanc Mortgage Corporation, Pat was a salesman. I should be clear here: calling him a salesman would have been like calling Superman a police officer. I mean, Pat could sell ice to Eskimos. And he sold me on HomeBanc. He told me he had followed my career and that he was looking for leaders, not just mortgage people. The offer that followed felt too good to be true. The company would buy my house, give me a six-figure salary, and move me to Tampa. Pat would teach me the business.

Since I felt like a drowning man looking for a lifeboat. I thought, *Why not try this? I can always go back to coaching.* I bought into what Pat Flood was selling!

After training at HomeBanc, I went to work in Tampa. That had been the plan. They bought my house in Cincinnati, I planted roots in Tampa, and I never went back to coaching.

When people ask how and why I left coaching, I tell them I tried to stay in coaching, but God put Pat into my life because he had other plans for me.

I do know that if I would have stayed in Cincinnati with Dick LeBeau and remained in coaching, my life would have been completely different today.

The coaching profession is a selfish profession, particularly where family is concerned. You get promoted or fired, and you move on to the next stop. The coach goes to work with people he or she probably knows or has coached with in the past. The family is left to uproot from friends and support mechanisms, as well as from people you count on every day, like doctors, dentists, barbers, and hairdressers. I think it's a lot like the military personnel way of life.

Leaving coaching afforded me more time with my family. In the spring of 1998 while in training for HomeBanc in Atlanta, Mary Gayle became pregnant. Our second child, Andrew Parker Phillips, surprised us by arriving early on January 5, 1999, which happened to be my birthday. What a birthday present, by far the best I ever received! With all that we had been through, we were truly blessed with God's gift of our second child.

All felt right with the world, including my departure from the profession I loved.

I did manage to look in the rearview mirror and saw that I had been blessed with many great players and great coaches during my career. More important, they were all great people.

Thanks to those people, once in business, I found that coaching and recruiting had brought me a solid foundation for learning how to manage people in regard to process and strategy. I am convinced that many of my successes in business and life have been a result of my foundation of thoughts and processes that the coaching profession instilled in me for thirteen years.

Lou Holtz treated his position like he was the CEO of a business. Basically, he had ten guys sitting around the table, and each person had an obligation to execute their duties. He laid out the strategies, and each coach had a defined role in the organization. And he held you accountable.

Following Coach Holtz's example, I intentionally surrounded myself with smarter people than myself when I got to HomeBanc. I laid out the strategy and tried to hold them accountable while I coached them through the process.

I knew I could push and lead people. I also needed help,

because I had a recognizable deficiency of knowledge of the mortgage business, since I hadn't come up through the ranks in the business. I got really lucky, with a particularly good operations person in Jo Wall.

Jo had started way back as a receptionist at Ryan Homes in Virginia and had grown her career, including a stint where she had worked for Fannie Mae. She knew the business backward and forward. Having Jo allowed me to concentrate on marketing, to get out and do what I do best. And that strategy worked.

Getting back on the golf course more frequently proved to be one of the nicer offshoots of becoming a businessman. I'd always enjoyed golf, and suddenly I found myself playing with customers and building relationships while out on the course. Such outings helped my business immeasurably. Having a football background helped me connect, too. There are a lot of people who enjoy talking football with somebody who has been on the inside of the sport.

In business—no matter what business you're in—having the ability to close means everything. Fortunately, I've been a good closer, another quality I learned from Dad.

I think part of my ability to close came organically from watching Dad when I would accompany him to work. His engagement and his salesmanship when he talked with employees and prospective clients gave me a solid foundation for closing.

Of course, in football, recruiting is all about closing—finding ways to get parents and players to buy into what you were trying to sell. Also, in the off-season you have to go to booster and alumni functions. Those experiences afforded me the opportunity to meet leaders in the business world and learn from them.

I strongly believe that people do business with people whom they like. And if you can establish that you're trustworthy and honest, then people will give you a chance.

Realtors and builders drive a bulk of the mortgage business. We marketed to them. We were a really top-notch marketing machine with excellent customer service. We built key relationships with many happy hours, drinks, and dinners. We did whatever we needed to do.

Being successful in business also brought out the competitor in me.

Coaching involves getting athletes to practice preparing them to perform on game day. I had been selling something every day. Business is the same way. You surround the players/employees with support and personnel to help them achieve. You give them sound game plans for success. Also, in this process, you care for, you motivate, and you nurture. Not only do you want to see the players or associates be successful on the field, but also you want to see them be as successful off the field, or away from the office and giving back to their local communities.

During my years in business, I've recruited, hired, motivated, developed strategy, and been a psychologist and counselor while trying to help the company be successful and helping my associates achieve their goals in life.

Early in my professional career, I developed a personal mission statement: "If I can help people get what they want in life. . . then I will get what I need."

No doubt, I experienced a period of adjustment. Like the nature of the calendar. I did the same amount of work in business that I did while coaching, but the workload was spread out over a longer period of time.

When I coached, July and August were really busy, then the season started and my hours remained intense before easing up in January.

During the weeks, in the NFL, you are packed in on Monday through Thursday, with Friday and Saturday being very light days.

In college, you were packed in from Sunday through Thursday, too. And you had to sandwich recruiting visits into the equation, too.

Once I began at HomeBanc, I continued to arrive to work early, and I still worked late, but all of my work wasn't compacted into a six- or seven-month span.

I didn't really think about it while I was coaching in college— and I probably would have been a nervous wreck if I had—but my livelihood depended to a large extent on the performances of kids who were eighteen to twenty-one. At the time, I think I just considered it part of the gig. I didn't think about all the changes that were going on in a kid of that age. Succeeding in football was just a part of who they were, and their performances, the performances that affected my livelihood, could be altered by breaking up with a girlfriend, or having bad news from home.

The NFL brought a little different climate, which obviously was more business-like. The players were older, they were paid a lot of money, and they knew they were paid to perform, like a business. But when you cut to the chase, your livelihood still depended on young men and their performances during a sixty-minute game. Even the smart players make dumb decisions on the football field from time to time. Sometimes you'd shake your head and wonder why in the world a player had done something so stupid. But the game moves fast. Decisions have to be made in a split second. That kind of pressure makes for a lot of bad decisions. Coaches get blamed for those decisions, and, ultimately, those decisions can cost a coach his job.

Dealing with females in the workplace actually presented me one of the more difficult transitions when I left coaching. Coaches are dirty sailors. Once in the workplace, I had to alter my vocabulary. Instead of an F-bomb, you had to be more like Bobby Bowden. "Dad-gummit, why'd you do that?"

In addition, business had a different dress code. Early in my business career, you had to wear a suit and tie, whereas now, many companies and industries have turned to business casual as everyday dress. At Notre Dame, we wore shirts and ties during the season, then dressed down a little bit after the season. Coaches' shirts were acceptable at LSU. And in the NFL, you threw on a pair of warmups and a sweatshirt and walked out the door. In the banking and finance world, you might have an occasional casual day here or there, but generally, you're mandated to wear a coat and tie most days.

I don't have any doubt that I would have had my share of successes in business if I had not coached first. But I do feel strongly that it would have been more difficult and certainly not as fulfilling.

Whether you're a player, a coach, a businessman, or a parent, success comes down to coaching someone—helping someone be better than what they are, or to be the best they can be. In essence, most of my life has been centered around coaching in some shape or form.

I've realized that I received quality coaching early in my life, and a lot of the lessons I learned carried over. Going as far back as being on Carol City's Little League All-Star team, I experienced top-shelf coaching from Ron Cussins and Dale Shields.

Those guys had me starting at second base and leading off, creating a situation for me that could have been overwhelming, since I was just eleven at the time (most of my teammates were twelve). In 1974, Carol City had a competitive Little League that had won several championships and one Junior Little League world championship. Coach Cussins and Coach Shields must have recognized some quality in me, because they told me to be a leader. They helped me build my leadership foundation. Then they guided me and ingrained in me some of the leadership basics that still hold true while doing what I do every day. Things you can control: be on time, stay late, get in front of the line, do little things, and have fun.

As a player, coach, or businessman, you usually don't realize how the coaches and people around you have influenced you until you leave them. Only then can you gain a perspective—good or bad— based upon those influences and experiences.

Funny how a lot of the things I learned from coaches were the same things my dad tried to teach me. But sometimes a son just needs to hear a different voice from his father's, because "he's just Dad."

It certainly goes both ways, too. When Trent, my older son, played YMCA eight-man football at eight years old, I tried to help him learn how to play quarterback. That became a frustrating experience for both of us, because it didn't matter how many tips I gave him, or how good those tips were: what I said wasn't sinking in. I wasn't getting through to him. Finally, I asked him if he would listen if I brought Jon Gruden out to help him. Gruden coached the Tampa Bay Buccaneers at the time.

Trent's response: "Sure!"

I proceeded to ask the next question: "Why would you listen to Jon Gruden?"

Trent didn't hesitate with his answer. "Because he's coached in the NFL."

I continued. "Well, what did Dad do before he worked at HomeBanc?"

Trent answered, "You coached in the NFL."

I moved to my conclusion. "So why don't you listen to me?"

To him, the answer was simple: "Because you're Dad!"

I guess some things a son can only hear from Dad, but only understand from others!

CHAPTER 20

Rediscovering White Fang

MORE FAMILY TIME RANKED AT the top of the list of added benefits from leaving the coaching profession. In addition to the time I got to spend with Mary Gayle and our young children, moving back to Florida and being a businessman created more time for me to spend with Dad.

While I'd been away from Florida for thirteen years, I'd been back to my home state for recruiting visits on many occasions, particularly the Tampa Bay area, which ranked as a hotbed for football talent. Having recruited there allowed me to grow familiar with the Cigar City. I knew the area would be a great place to live. And living there turned out to be everything I had hoped it would be, particularly given the proximity to Dad.

Being able to observe Dad mellow with age brought me a warm feeling. As I've said, he had always preached about not sweating the small stuff. Even though that sounded nice, Dad in fact always did sweat the small stuff. All perfectionists do. I guess the older we get, the more we realize the small stuff isn't as big as we made it out to be. Dad got in the habit of making a lot of visits to Tampa. My mother rarely accompanied him. She did not share his enthusiasm about driving or flying from Miami to Tampa, even though the distance isn't great by either plane or car. She actually got sedentary the older she got, which made traveling more difficult for her and, therefore, curbed her enthusiasm to do so. Dad, on the other hand, would always be up for a trip.

Other than visits with the grandkids, golf would be the big magnet for both of us when Dad traveled to Tampa. He loved playing at the Avila Golf and Country Club, my home course in Tampa at the time.

Though Dad and I had not physically been together that much prior to my leaving the coaching profession, we'd been together a lot over the years in conversations, thoughts, and prayers. Many times, life's struggles had brought us together through all the disappointments, the ups and the downs. He had always been there for me to serve as a sounding board or dispatch sound advice. During those times when I had been struggling, he often told me, "Son, you are behind a few, and ahead of most in this world!" To this day, I use this saying a lot. I think it helps me and others understand how good life in the United States is for us as compared to other places in the world.

During one of Dad's trips to Tampa, we were sitting around my house, and the old Bull's Eye putter caught his attention. He asked me where I'd gotten the putter. While I told him, he examined the putter, noticing flecks of white paint on the flange during his inspection. He vaguely remembered a story about Jack Nicklaus and the fact he had not been able to locate two of his famous putters, one of them being a Bull's Eye known as "White Fang." Through our conversation, the seed got planted that I might be in possession of one of Nicklaus's prized missing putters.

I didn't think too much about our conversation until I was invited to Steve Nicklaus's 40th birthday party that had been scheduled to take place on April 12, 2003.

Traveling and coaching football for all those years after I got out of college didn't help me stay close to many of my friends in college. That was more my fault than that of any of my friends. Steve and I frequently stayed in touch over the years, so I felt good to be included on his invite list for the memorable occasion.

Steve had worked for the LPGA Tour when he first graduated from FSU. Certain staff members always went ahead to the next Tour stop to help get things prepared. Steve had been a part of one of those teams. On one occasion, he had been at a stop in Hattiesberg, Mississippi, and he planned on driving to Baton Rouge on a Sunday to see me. That was, of course, to take place on April 13, 1986, which turned out to be the weekend Jack brought down the house at Augusta National. At the age of forty-six, Jack won The Masters, making him the oldest to ever win the hallowed tournament. Instead of stopping in Baton Rouge, Steve adjusted his plans to be with Jack on that magical weekend.

Once the invitation to Steve's party arrived, I began to entertain the idea of bringing along the putter to the party to see what Jack thought of it. What sealed the deal was a business trip to Augusta with a title company to watch The Masters practice rounds at Augusta the week of Steve's party.

During Tuesday's practice round, Jack had just finished playing No. 17 and had started to make his way to No. 18 when I yelled out to him. He stopped, and we spoke briefly.

"Joe, what are you doing here?" he said.

I could feel all eyes on me, like, "Who the heck is this guy that Jack Nicklaus stopped to talk to in the middle of his practice round?"

I explained to him why I was there. Once he began to walk away, I said, "Jack, I hope I don't see you this weekend."

Initially, the remark seemed to catch him off guard. He quickly recovered, and he said, "Yeah I hope I don't see you, either."

If Jack made the cut for the weekend rounds of the tournament, he wouldn't be able to attend Steve's birthday party that Saturday night.

On my trip home from Augusta, I couldn't get my mind off that Bull's Eye putter. I don't know what came over me, but my gut told me I needed to bring along the putter with me to South Florida for Steve's party.

Fortunately for me, Jack missed the cut. That allowed him to attend the party.

When I saw him that Saturday night, I grinned and said, "I'm sorry to see that you're here tonight."

He smiled and agreed, though I'm sure he had mixed emotions. The consummate competitor living in him wanted to compete for another major title, while the consummate family man wanted to be around for a special family moment.

I introduced Mary Gayle to Jack. Everybody wanted to speak to Jack, which I'm sure brought a familiar scene. Talking to everybody and making everybody feel comfortable was just a part of who he was. He had begun to make his move to mingle with other party guests when I said, "Jack, I may have a club that might be yours!"

I had piqued his interest.

He said, "Well go get it, and we can talk about it."

Mary Gayle needed to retrieve her purse from the car anyway, so she offered to get the putter. When she returned, she handed over the Bull's Eye, which I passed along to Jack. Did this mysterious putter have an historical story?

Jack began to inspect the putter, examining every inch of the club from top to bottom. At one point, he closed his eyes and started moving the putter back and forth like a pendulum as if putting an imaginary ball. I began to wonder if he was reliving some great moment from the past that he might have had with this putter. His expression conveyed disbelief, like he couldn't believe what he held in his hands.

"Where have you had this?" Jack asked me.

I told him I'd been moved many times to various coaching stops and that I'd bunched the putter with an old set of wooden-shafted clubs my dad had given me. "They've been sitting on a shelf."

Jack smiled. "Do you know how much this is worth?"

I shrugged, offering a tentative laugh. "I have no idea. But by the sound of your voice, I would guess a couple hundred thousand?"

Jack didn't hesitate with his response. "No. Times that by five. I won the 1967 U.S. Open at Baltusrol with this putter!"

I continued to stand with Jack for much of the evening. I observed when old friends stopped to talk to him. When they saw the putter, several remarked, "That's White Fang, where did you get that?"

Even Barbara, Jack's wife, said, "That's White Fang. I used to spray-paint that in the parking lot!"

I learned that when needed, Barbara would spray-paint the head of the putter white to prevent the sun from reflecting off the putter, which might have been a distraction. Talk about the extra things a wife does for her husband!

The beat-up putter in his hands had matured to a worn shade of gold, yet it had a small speck of white paint clinging to the inner-most portion of the hook flange in the back end. The grip proved to be the characteristic of the putter that confirmed without a doubt that Jack had been reunited with an old friend.

PGA Tour players could once alter the grips any way they wanted. Jack had stuck a pencil in the back of the putter grip, then tape-wrapped the handle and broke the pencil. To everyone's surprise, now nearly forty years later, the pencil remained lodged in the back of the handle.

Jack glowed with White Fang in his hands. Finally, he turned to me with a childlike grin. "Well, can I have it?"

That made me smile. I'm thinking that the greatest golfer who has ever lived has just asked me if I would return a putter that had been his. I told him, "Of course, it's yours, you can have it."

The rest of the night was filled with taking pictures and enjoying the stories of Jack's triumphs and disappointments using White Fang. Eventually, Jack turned to me and said, "Joe, send me your specs, and I'll send you a set of clubs."

To this day, I don't know why or how I came up with my response. I do thank the Lord that I did. I looked at him and put my hand on his shoulder. "You're not getting off that easy."

He shot me a pensive look, and I continued, "You get Steve, and I'll get my Dad. Let's go to Augusta, and we will call it even."

Jack turned to Steve and said, "Book it. Let's go this fall."

Thus, a dream father/son golf trip was scheduled for October 21, 2003.

What a fun night. I'll never forget how happy Jack seemed to be. He later told writers about being reunited with White Fang: "It was Steve's birthday that night, but I am the one who got the best present."

Dad would have disagreed.

When I called Dad later that night, he couldn't believe he would be playing Augusta National in October. Not to mention the fact that he would be playing with his son and The Golden Bear, the golfer who had won The Masters Tournament six times. And all because of a putter called "White Fang"!

CHAPTER 21

East Lake, then First Taste of Augusta National

DAD AND I TALKED OFF and on throughout the summer of 2003 about our upcoming date at Augusta National with Jack and Steve Nicklaus. After speaking with Steve and Jack's assistant late that summer, we agreed on the details of the trip. October 21, 2003, could not come quickly enough.

Finally, the date came.

Our arrangements were set for Augusta. However, that would come after we enjoyed the first part of the day's two-part adventure: a golf excursion to Atlanta's East Lake Golf Club, the place where Bobby Jones had learned to play.

We flew from Miami to Atlanta and drove to East Lake to play a morning round at the historic golf course with my friend Jeff Morris and his father-in-law, Jerry Brannon. Jeff had played baseball at the University of South Carolina, and he'd been the person who served as my mentor and teacher when I joined HomeBanc.

Shortly after moving through the gates, we found ourselves in a time warp. In front of us, Bobby Jones appeared to be preparing to tee off for the final round of the U.S. Amateur. Dressed in knickers, shirt and tie, and sweater vest, Jones had a natty appearance and carried himself—perhaps unsurprisingly—with an air of confidence.

Two dozen spectators were in attendance. Among the group were several little boys watching "Bobby"—better known to moviegoers as Jim Caviezel—idolizing every move and mannerism. The sparkle in their eyes said, "Maybe one day I can be like him."

Dad and I made our way through the clubhouse, taking time to look at all the memorabilia, trophies, medals, and pins. After we put on our shoes, we were ready to play. Once outside again, we were privy to watching Bobby Jones finish his round on the No. 18, a 235-yard par 3. A small lake and two wicked traps protected the finishing hole. Bobby hit the tee shot with the grace and fluid movement depicted in the pictures and books I'd read over the years. The ball arched toward the green and bounced off the wicker basket at the top of the pin. Everyone cheered when the ball landed two feet from the hole, assuring Bobby of another U.S. Open (amateur) title.

Dad and I turned and walked off that green, amazed at what we'd seen. We'd be teeing off in thirty minutes, so we had to warm up. Before we did, we stopped and complimented the director of the upcoming movie, "Bobby Jones: Stroke of Genius," starring Caviezel. I told him it was a shame we couldn't have the cameras follow us, letting him know about our golf date with a golfer of Bobby Jones's stature. The director smiled and asked us where our round with Jack Nicklaus would take place. I told him we would be playing at a little golf course about two hours east of where we stood, at a place that Bobby Jones built called Augusta National, home of The Masters Tournament.

Teeing off, we couldn't help but feel the presence of many of golf's greatest stars. The day was beautiful and the golf was fun, but we had to catch a plane. Our much-anticipated date with the Golden Bear sat on the horizon.

We met Jack at the Peachtree Dekalb Airport to take his private jet to Augusta.

As we entered the airport, my expectations and feelings about the trip were starting to build. The G-4 jet we boarded had #N1 JN painted on the tail. That helped me realize that the dream of playing Augusta National for the first time, and with my father, would become a reality. Never mind that we were preparing to play the course with Jack Nicklaus.

Jack had just bought the Gulfstream V from an oil company's CEO. When we walked up the stairs to board, a big Golden Bear logo stared back at us from the walnut panel at the entrance to the plane. I felt like they were filming an episode of *Lifestyles of the Rich and Famous* and I had been picked to be a part of the episode.

We exchanged pleasantries with Jack upon boarding the aircraft. While this wasn't the first time I'd been around Jack, it was the first time I'd had him to myself to ask questions. I admired him so much that I wanted to learn more about him.

When Steve and I were roommates, I used to badger him all the time: "Do you realize who your father is? He's probably one of the most well-known people in the world. Forget sports people. Just people in general. Even nongolfers know who Jack Nicklaus is."

Gracious as always, Jack was interested in catching up with what I was doing, too. He remained a huge fan of Ohio State, so the Buckeyes were part of the conversation, along with the Bengals and the time I'd spent coaching there.

Before I knew it, we had puddle-jumped to Augusta, grabbed a car at the airport, and driven directly to Augusta National.

Pulling up to Magnolia Lane, we stopped at the security gate. Jack began digging into his pocket to find his driver's license to show the guard, who smiled back at him.

"Mr. Nicklaus, I know who you are. I think you're okay."

Once we got settled into Firestone Cabin, where we would stay for the next two days, Jack asked us what we wanted to do. I answered: "We didn't come here to play Pinochle."

"Let's go lace 'em up," he said.

First, we hit some balls on the plushest driving range I had ever been on, then we headed for the nine-hole, par-3 course. Fifteen years later, Jack would get moved to tears on that same course.

Flash-forward for a moment.

During the 2018 Masters Par-3 Contest on the Wednesday before the tournament, Jack played with Gary Player and Tom Watson. None of what that fabled group did that day caught any-body's attention, though. Rather, it was what G.T. Nicklaus did that wowed the crowd. Jack's grandson, and the son of Gary Nicklaus, caddied for Jack that day. Wearing the white caddy coveralls, G.T. took aim at the pin at No. 9. And he drained it.

Jack teared up when speaking about how special it had been to see his fifteen-year-old grandson make his first-ever hole in one, especially given the fact that he'd done so at Augusta National. Jack called it "perhaps" his most memorable day at Augusta National.

That's Jack Nicklaus, the father and grandfather.

Back to our moment in 2003, though. Since the light disappears quickly in October, we had a sense of urgency to get going so we could finish our round. Two caddies joined us as we powered over to the first tee.

You can't understand the typography of this nine-hole, par-3 course just by watching the tournament on TV. Venturing onto the course is like descending into a big bowl.

Jack suggested that Dad and he would play Steve and me for ten dollars per man. I laughed, since Dad always told me, "It's not always how you play, it's the partner you pick."

In that vein, Dad did just fine that day.

Jack had missed birdie putts on the first two holes and faced a twelve-foot birdie putt on No. 3. Steve sidled next to me while his father lined up his putt. "He won't miss this f***ing putt."

Sure enough, he knocked it in.

When we walked off the green, Steve elaborated: "When he misses two in a row, he's won't miss the next one."

We both laughed.

Steve was out there cutting up. What he said about his dad just showed how much time he'd spent around him and how frequently he'd seen him play golf.

As for my own father-son dynamic that day, I had my moment when I caught the glow on Dad's face. I couldn't help thinking about what was going on in his head—he, a World War II veteran who had played golf at many great courses over the years, and now he was playing a par-3 at the greatest golf venue in the world, and his partner is arguably the greatest golfer to ever play the game.

Steve and I were closed out on our $10 bet after the eighth hole, which prompted some banter.

"Look Jack, I only have a twenty, so I'm going to give you the twenty, and you're going to sign it and give it back to me," I said.

The competitor in Jack chirped back. "Like hell I'm going to do that. I'm taking the twenty, I'm going to change it, then I'm going to sign the ten and give it back to you."

The $10 bill he handed back to me read: "Joe, how 'lucky' can you get Jack Nicklaus," and he dated the bill.

The longest hole on the par-3 course required me to hit a 7-iron. Watching the highlights of the par-3 tournament held at The Masters, I always got the feeling that playing that hole would be easy, as if they were throwing darts at the pin. Playing the course brought me more respect for what the PGA Tour players do, making that hole look easy. That's why they're the best golfers in the world.

We showered after the round and dressed in coats and ties for dinner.

As the sun set, I stood on the back porch of the Firestone Cabin looking over the fairway and pinching myself. Was I really currently living a longtime dream come to fruition? Yes, came the answer to my question. I was filled with the same excitement I felt on Christmas Eve as a kid. On top of that, Dad and I were about to have dinner with the man who had won The Masters six times. All because I kept a putter he used to win a U.S. Open.

We walked across the 10th tee and the practice putting green to the clubhouse dining room. As I trailed behind Jack, I continued to pinch myself, so I took a picture just in case I woke up.

Jack wore his green jacket. I learned that all winners wear a green jacket, not just during the Champions Dinner. Jack cut a gracious figure to all tables in the dining room, walking around and greeting many of those dining. He signed autographs and took pictures with anyone who asked.

We talked about the different tournaments and memorable moments he had had at Augusta National. Throughout the night, Jack acted like a curator for Augusta while he explained the different details of every nook and cranny of the fabled club. I wish I had recorded it. I felt like I was visiting an historical shrine or monument. Many can come and see what we saw from the outside, but very few get to see it from the inside. Only a handful get to experience it with one of the people who has helped build Augusta National's aura and reputation over the years. I felt like a student in a classroom listening to a wise college professor.

Jack said he thought President Dwight D. Eisenhauer painted the two portraits—of Bobby Jones and Clifford Roberts, who was the first chairman of Augusta National (1931–1976)—that hung in the dining room.

Following dinner, Jack guided us through the main room where The Masters Trophy is housed. We saw the Champions Locker Room, where he shares a locker with Horton Smith, who won the tournament in 1934 and again in 1936, then headed to the "Crow's Nest," where he stayed in 1958 with Bill Rogers. He told us the story that after the second day, a tournament official came up and told Rogers and him that they would have to charge them an "extra dollar" a day because they were eating so much. Jack told them that would be fine.

We went into the members' locker room, where Jack has another locker that he shares with Hugh McColl, the former CEO and Chairman of Bank of America. Jack's many stories about what makes Augusta National so mythical made for a special evening.

We returned to Firestone Cabin to watch Game 3 of the World Series between the Florida Marlins and the New York Yankees. All of us were tired, so everyone turned in about 11 o'clock.

I knew Dad had to be exhausted from walking the hills. He fell asleep quickly. Meanwhile, I found myself too amped up to sleep. I grabbed a book and camped out on the back porch, savoring my surroundings. I stared through the pine trees at a fall moon that illuminated the 10th fairway. I could not help but question myself, *Now how did you get here again? How is it that one day in college you tossed your putter up to a green while waiting to chip? When you went to putt, you then realized you'd broken your putter!* One simple toss—an action performed daily by many golfers—led to a sequence of future events and decisions that resulted in me being here on this back porch and about to play Augusta with Jack Nicklaus.

I continued to reflect. If I had thrown out some junk clubs in any of the many moves I'd made, this fortuitous opportunity would never have arisen. Add to that the fate of being paired with a roommate in college who turned out to be Jack Nicklaus's son. I thought of all the great golf courses I'd been fortunate enough to play. In the rearview mirror, I saw St. Andrews, Oak Hill, Pine Valley, Pebble Beach, Muirfield Village, Turnberry, Westchester, Winged Foot, Doral, Troon, Prestwick, Pinehurst No. 2, Bay Hill, Olympic, East Lake, Shoal Creek, Whistling Straits, and even Country Club of Miami, where my love affair with golf was born.

No book, no fishing tale, and no movie could make this up. I'm so thankful I broke my putter.

To borrow an expression from the Golden Bear, "How lucky can you get?"

CHAPTER 22

Golfing with the Golden Bear at Augusta National

Talk about golf heaven, that's where I resided when I awakened on October 22, 2003, in the Firestone Cabin, just off Augusta National's No. 10 fairway.

Any weather concerns were quickly put to rest the second I popped my head out from the porch. Not a cloud in the sky. Only the noise of the wind whistling through the pines could be heard. The pristine, immaculate grass had a sheen. Just a gorgeous setting. Azaleas in full bloom were the only missing ingredient. Alas, fall is not a time for flowers.

Loving golf like I do, I get excited if I'm headed to the golf course to meet my buddies for a Saturday morning round. Multiply that by about a million, and you could understand what I felt that morning.

I'd been to Augusta National to watch The Masters, but I'd never played the big course (after all, the "little course" the day before had merely been an appetizer of sorts). Doing so would be the equivalent of playing football at Lambeau Field, basketball at the Boston Garden, or baseball at Fenway Park. And I'd be playing my first round at golf's most storied course with Jack Nicklaus, arguably the greatest golfer to ever swing a club, sharing the experience with my father and my college roommate.

The script unfolding in front of me felt surreal. Only it wasn't.

In my mind, I'd gone over every detail of the coming day. I'd even laid out my clothes the night before. I felt like I was getting dressed for New Year's Eve. In many ways, my behavior resembled that of a little girl excitedly prepping for a tea party. I settled on a white shirt, a sweater, a pair of khaki pants, and shoes that matched.

Dad, Steve, Jack, and I gathered in the living room of the cabin, then headed to the clubhouse restaurant for breakfast, passing the tee box for No. 10 and crossing through the putting green behind the clubhouse.

Jack walked in front of me, wearing a Golden Bear shirt and windbreaker. The fog inside my mind still had not lifted. *Are Dad and I really at Augusta National with Jack Nicklaus? Am I going to wake up? When is an alarm clock going to interrupt my dream?*

Dad had to be feeling the same way.

Normally, Dad would be gregarious. He'd carried a big outward personality everywhere he went his entire life. Not this day. He quietly went about his business, observing his surroundings and following the advice he'd given me years before about knowing my place. He stressed the wisdom of understanding who you were and what you were in relation to your setting.

The restaurant wasn't pretentious. Nothing really distinguished the place from any other clubhouse restaurant I'd been to, other than the clubs. Sets of clubs and individual clubs from past champions were prominently displayed on the walls along with plaques and photos. I glanced at the walls during our leisurely breakfast of eggs, sausage, and bacon.

Jack continued to play the gracious host, telling us how he thought our visit was a great thing and how he was glad the outing had come together. I think he had the same kind of relationships with Steve and the rest of his children, so he understood some of what we were experiencing.

The restaurant staff cooed over Jack, which didn't surprise me—he was Jack Nicklaus. Nor did he surprise me how cordial and polite he treated them in return. I don't know if it's the uniqueness of golf, or the type of people who play the sport, but as a group, the golfers who played on the PGA Tour have always seemed to realize that the fans were the people who supported them. Not only from a personality standpoint—fulfilling their egos—but they also supported them financially. PGA Tour professionals know they have a responsibility to themselves and to the group of individuals against whom they competed each week to conduct themselves accordingly.

Football players don't always think that way.

Individualization is downplayed in team sports, and I think that affects how they treat fans and people around them. Whereas in the golf and the tennis worlds—and in the world of bowling and any other individual sport for that matter—the athletes realize that the fans are superimportant.

Jack was polite and cordial, but that didn't mean he couldn't let his hair down and be himself. I think he understood that people naturally were on edge around him because of his status. He put us at ease. I didn't feel much different from how I would have felt getting ready to play a round with my regular golf group—until I reminded myself that I was about to play Augusta National for the first time with a man who'd won The Masters six times.

After breakfast, we met our caddies. Mine told me he'd been there almost twenty years. I don't remember his name, but he was witty and was good reading putts. As I walked down the hill on the dogleg left ninth hole, I asked what he did when the course was closed. He looked at me with a perplexed smile. "I collect unemployment."

I told him the story about how I had been on unemployment my first year at Notre Dame. He got a chuckle out of that. I don't imagine many who have played Augusta National have drawn unemployment checks.

We loosened up at the driving range, which had a net up against a fence. I had to try and be a macho man by driving the fence.

Who was I impressing? Jack Nicklaus had been the best golfer in the world, and he'd played with all the other top golfers, too. Pretty silly of me.

Ever the classy guy, Jack didn't say anything. After all, I was one of his guests. Civility and cordiality were from another era. He aspired to both.

On the putting green trying to get a feel for the greens with my flavor-of-the-month high-tech putter, I ventured back in time and thought about White Fang. I remembered using that Bull's Eye putter on the FSU golf course, and it felt as though I were putting with a butter knife. Technology-wise, using that putter today would be like pulling out a persimmon wood and trying to hit a 275-yard drive. I enjoyed a silent chuckle thinking, *I'm here because I didn't throw that putter away.*

We ran into David Frost when walking back from the range. We talked with him for about ten minutes before we arrived at the first tee for our 10 a.m. tee time. Frost would be playing in a group behind us. There were only about four or five groups playing that day.

Throughout my sports life, I've been fortunate in that I've always been able to manage my nerves well regardless of what sport I played, at least to the point where my performance wasn't affected. Although Augusta National was the Holy Grail, my experiences from eighteen years of playing and coaching football, and being in different venues, helped me relax. The only time I flirted with nervousness came when I stuck the peg in the ground on the first tee, hoping I could put one safely into the fairway.

The first hole is a 445-yard par 4 known as "Tea Olive." Each hole on the par-72 course has a name that is derived from the flora found on the hole.

We hit from an elevated tee across an expansive valley toward a tree-lined fairway with a deep bunker on the right.

I striped my drive down the middle, short of the bunker.

Jack and Steve hit, then Dad, who played from the front tees. While I had battled a few nerves, for some reason I felt even more nervous for Dad. On the one hand, I knew he had to be feeling a little bit jelly-legged thinking about making solid contact and playing well. On the other hand, I also knew his life experiences had equipped him to handle this. He'd been around movie stars, singers, and actors, and he played a lot of tournament golf in Pro-Ams and at the Country Club of Miami with professional athletes and celebrities.

He successfully launched his tee shot down the fairway, and we were underway for our eighteen-hole walk into golf heaven.

Jack picked out the tees we played on every hole. We didn't go back to the tips on any of them. We played farther back on the twelfth and sixteenth holes, but for the most part, we played the midback tees. Dad played the front tees the entire round. A couple of times during the round, I told Jack I wanted to play from the back tees, but he vetoed that option.

"No, let's play it from here," Jack said.

Truth be told, I don't think he wanted to walk all the way to the back tees, which can require a little hike.

At sixty-three, Jack could still hit the ball a lot like Jack Nicklaus, and he still played competitive professional golf, though you got the idea he wasn't going to be one of those professional golfers who played until he could no longer draw his club back. Point being, once Jack stepped onto the golf course, whether he hit practice balls or played a round, the competitive juices came to him, and he wanted to perform well.

No telling how many rounds Jack had logged in his life, but he wasn't just going through the motions with us. He remained engaged. He was very deliberate in his shots. His routine, though probably a bit faster than normal, was still pure Jack Nicklaus. He would line up his shot, pick out a spot five to six feet in front of his ball, address the ball, and swing. Everything we'd seen him do on TV thousands of times.

When we reached each hole, Jack gave us some help, offering a scouting report, then he would remind himself about what he wanted to do with the ball. He'd say things, like, "I've got to draw this in and hit it on the top shelf here."

Whether Jack felt like being out there competing with us or not, he gave the impression he cared about the round. This despite the fact that he was still playing "real" rounds. In fact, he had just played his final U.S. Senior Open that June, and he'd played in his last Senior British Open that July, finishing 25th and 14th, respectively.

Jack hit a shot on No. 10 that stood out.

Known as Camelia, the par-four, 495-yard tenth hole had been the opening hole at Augusta National prior to 1935. Jack told us that you needed to hit a draw to best take advantage of the downhill fairway. Of course, I flared mine into the trees to the right. He then addressed his ball and executed his shot to perfection, drawing his 3-wood into the downhill trough. A shot like that offered an exclamation point about who we were playing with. I can't guess how many times he had hit that shot over the hundreds of rounds he had played there.

Steve was great, too. We picked up right where we'd left off, always jabbing each other. We didn't get a bet going, because, like always, he had a hard time giving strokes. He'd always say, "You don't get any shots, play better." He thought my handicap was too high.

Augusta National easily ranks as the most well-kept course I've ever played. That could be attributed to the fact it's only open for play twice a year during periods in the spring and the fall.

No matter where you hit the ball, it's sitting up as if it's on a tee when you get there. You just don't get a bad lie, even in the rough. If you hit it into the pine straw, it sits up there, too. That gives you all kinds of confidence. The rough doesn't penalize you, either. I mean, there are no areas that are bad. Even if you hit a bad shot, you have a chance to get it out. If they had normal greens, good golfers would torch that golf course. Basically, you earn your score on your ability to chip and putt.

Playing with somebody of Jack's stature, any golfer would wonder what he thought of their swing. I wasn't thinking that way. I knew that the last thing he wanted to do was tinker with my swing if not asked to do so. Well, maybe. Jack did offer some advice during the round.

I'd been spraying my tee ball to the right, and he finally grew tired of watching me do so. He told me, "If you're going to hook the ball, get on the left-hand side of the tee box. You fade the ball, get over on the right side."

His other comment came late in the round after I missed a green to the right. "Always aim more to the left. When your legs get tired, aim left."

So, he coached me up whether I wanted it or not. He couldn't help himself.

Playing with Jack felt a lot like throwing the football with Earl Morrall or Bob Griese in high school. They made me feel like I was playing with one of my uncles. Jack did the same, helping me to forget I was playing with a golf superhero. All of those guys could tell you what to do and give you tips. Yet when they did what they did compared to what you did, they were effortless and efficient, putting on display why they were professionals.

Dad and Jack got along fine, too.

Dad would ask him about some of the older golfers he could relate to like Gay Brewer, Lee Trevino, and Chi Chi Rodriguez.

That triggered stories, and they'd banter about some of the older golf courses in the Miami, Fort Lauderdale, and West Palm Beach areas, some of them no longer in existence.

Because Dad played from the front tees, he stayed off to the side while we hit. He wanted to follow golf etiquette to the tee, which might have bogged him down a little bit. Nobody likes playing with a slow golfer, and Dad might have been a little too deliberate. I hoped that wasn't wearing on Jack's and Steve's nerves.

But the Nicklaus duo seemed to play it cool. Jack continued to explain things about each hole, delving into all the little idiosyncrasies of the hole as we moved up the fairway.

No. 11, for example, the par-four, 505-yard White Dogwood hole, was the first of the three holes forming "Amen Corner." It was on this hole that Larry Mize chipped in to defeat Greg Norman in a playoff for the 1987 title. Jack explained that the hole had been lengthened, and the trees along the right side kept you from bailing out. Because of the changes, the hole had become more difficult and forced players to play the hole more conservatively rather than taking chances to make shots.

Yet I'd conducted my own study of this course, as well—both from afar and in person. When we got to No. 8, an uphill par five known as Yellow Jasmine, I knew from my Masters research that Bruce Devlin had scored the second double eagle in Masters history on that hole in 1967. Of course, Gene Sarazen's "shot heard 'round the world" in 1935 was the first. Sarazen's took place on No. 15.

Navigating No. 8 required an accurate tee ball to avoid the fairway bunker on the right side. Mounds on the left protected a narrow green. I managed to hit a gap wedge tight and sank the putt for my only birdie of the day.

While walking down the No. 9 fairway, I shared with the group the story of the first time I went to The Masters to watch a practice round in 1990.

I'd seen Mark Lye on the third hole. My old friend had invited me to walk with him, so I did, studying the course and how he hit the shots he did. He pulled his tee shot on No. 9, and when he reached his ball, I could see that a pine tree blocked his way. I stood behind him, about ten feet away, and wondered what he would try to do with the ball. The whole time, I thought, *There's no way he's going to be able to hit the green. He can't get it out of there.*

Mark ended up hitting a 5-iron off the pine needles, threading his ball through a narrow opening in the trees to where it came to rest about fifteen feet from the hole. And he'd had no shot. Being there to see him pull his Houdini act amazed me. I remember playing Killearn Country Club in Tallahassee with him years before, and he did the same type of thing. Over the years, that is one thing I have learned from pro and low-handicap golfers. When they hit a bad shot and get into trouble, they know how to get out of trouble. The normal golfer isn't consistent enough—or patient enough—to follow the bad shot with a good one.

I didn't experience any trouble on No. 9 and came away with a par, leaving me with a three-over 39 for the front. Dad shot 47, Steve shot 39, and Jack shot 39, too, so I felt cocky, like, *This is pretty easy. I'm going toe-to-toe with Jack Nicklaus, the guy who won The Masters six times.*

My fortunes changed on the back side, thanks largely to a triple-bogey on the par three, No. 12. Troubles incurred on "Golden Bell" included dumping my tee ball into the water, then burying my next shot into the azaleas on the back side of the green.

During my reversal of fortunes, I did experience a moment of glory on No. 16.

I sprayed my tee shot to the right of the par three "Redbud," which is played entirely over water and features a large sloping green surrounded by deep bunkers. Jack observed my errant effort and noted, "Whoa, haven't seen too many people go over there."

The pin had been stationed deep on the upper right side of the green near a trap. On Sundays at The Masters, the pin is at located on the front left side, where even a good shot can trickle back into the water.

My ball rested on pine needles approximately twenty to thirty yards away. The chances of getting up and down were remote. I needed to land the ball over the trap and stop it on a dime to avoid sliding downhill toward the water. I grabbed my 60-degree wedge and thought, *What the hell.*

I made solid contact—a good first step. The ball popped into the air and stopped five feet from the pin. I sank the putt. *Ho hum,* routine par.

Walking to the next hole, my caddy told me, "Thanks boss, you just made me some money. The over/under was 6 for you." I was glad I could do my part to help him stay away from the unemployment line for another week.

Speaking of caddies, they know everything about that course, particularly the greens. On No. 18, I drove the ball into the trees on the right, leaving me without a shot. My caddy looked at me and said, "Shoot it on up there toward 10 tee."

I tried to do as instructed, but I pulled my shot. The ball ended up in the bunker on the right side of the No. 18 green.

Standing in the bunker lining my feet up to hit a shot to where I thought I needed to hit the ball, I looked up on the green at my caddy.

"Just hit it up here," he said.

He drew an imaginary circle at a target that didn't make sense. Following his instructions would mean hitting the ball north when the hole was southwest. I didn't question his judgement. I hit the ball where he told me, then marveled while it rolled to about three or four feet from the hole. Had I not experienced the shot, I never would have thought that was the way to play it.

I missed my putt to finish with a 47 on the back, giving me an

86 for the day. Jack shot 78, and Steve came in at 80. Dad shot 57 on the back for a 104.

Jack seemed a little disappointed with his score, much like a concerto pianist would be after hitting a couple of wrong notes.

We showered, packed up, and headed out of Magnolia Lane. Before we boarded the plane, Jack had some work to do at a new course that was under construction called Champions Retreat. That twenty-seven-hole venture was a collaborative design by Jack, Arnold Palmer, and Gary Player. Each of the golfing legends was tasked with designing nine holes. Ever the perfectionist, Jack wanted to take notes on the layout and observe the progress being made, so we tagged along with Jack and some of his people.

Walking the holes of that course with him and hearing his vision for each hole proved intriguing. Each hole already had been cut through the trees, and they were about to move a lot of dirt. As we got to one of the par 3s, we stood on the tee and looked over a small duck pond to an hourglass green on the other side. There were trees on the left along with the remnants of a duck blind in those trees. Jack blurted out, "What are we going to do with that?"

Silence followed. I broke that silence by suggesting he put a couple of dummies in the blind with fake shotguns and have decoys out in front of the blind. Jack turned to me and said, "That's a pretty good idea. Take note of that, guys." I never found out if my suggestion got put into place.

Afterward, we boarded Jack's jet to fly to West Palm. Jack was gracious enough to autograph several of his Precept balls that he played with during our Augusta round. During the flight, Dad went to the bathroom, and Jack told me, "Hey, your dad has to learn how to play a little quicker." That cracked me up.

When we landed, we came to a stop next to another plane in the hangar, N1GN. I knew we were in N1JN. Turned out, Jack's Gulfstream V shared the same hangar with Greg Norman's plane.

Like all great dreams, you don't want them to end. I was waiting for Dad to break out in song with "I Could Have Danced All Night" or "The Impossible Dream." We could have begged for more, but our impossible dream was now over! We said our good-byes before Dad and I took a taxi to Miami.

Riding on the Florida Turnpike, we passed Pro Player Stadium, where Game 4 of the World Series was taking place. I felt blessed to be able to appreciate how special our time together had been. We'd played golf and spent time with Jack Nicklaus at Augusta National. To top it all off, Dad's favorite baseball team was playing in the World Series, and the Marlins were taking it to the Yankees.

As we drove, tears formed in my eyes. Dad, at seventy-seven, would be the first to admit that his golf game wasn't what it used to be, yet his love for the game was stronger than ever. I couldn't help but think that if I were still coaching, I never would have been in the position to experience what we had just shared together.

Days later, I received the following note:

Dear Joe,

This by way of thanks and appreciation for the memorable Augusta trip. It was very considerate of you to think of me and include me. Everything, even the 103 score [note: Dad had himself down for one shot less], was awesome. When I think of all the golfers in the world who would give anything to do what I did with you, I'm so grateful and proud to have a son like you. But above all, I'm so proud of your accomplishments and thoughtfulness—not just this, but all the time. You've certainly made my last few birthdays something to remember.

Love always, Dad

CHAPTER 23

Papa Joe's Final Years

IN THE BIBLE, SOLOMON TELLS US that life is "meaningless" if we do not have our focus on God's word. Yet he also tells us to enjoy the life we are given. Louis Joseph Wessel lived under that guidance for 89 1/2 years. Many would say my father was a true Renaissance man as described in this definition of a Renaissance man, from Urban Dictionary: "a person who is 'enlightened' in all subject matter including arts, math, athletics, philosophy, music, history, and any other cultural aspect of society."

Dad knew it all and wasn't shy to share his knowledge. He was enlightened throughout his life, and the people who had the privilege of knowing him were enlightened because of him.

Dad's final years were peaceful. He remained sharp, with his sense of humor intact, and he'd sing us a tune every now and then.

Some people spend their whole lives searching for their purpose. Dad's purpose always seemed to come to him effortlessly and with clarity.

Dad sang in the choir, ushered at mass, helped the needy, and always gave advice, whether you sought his advice or not. He sold spices for McCormick for thirty-five years. And he loved to brag to people about the stock price.

Once Dad joined Alcoholics Anonymous, another purpose was born for him. Our Catholic Christian faith calls us to serve others. To reach out to those in need. For over forty years, Alcoholics Anonymous gave Dad the stage to fulfill that calling. Regardless of race, creed, or color, Dad embraced being a leader, sponsor, confidant, mentor, and friend to so many, unselfishly giving his time, his smile, his words of encouragement, and, every once in a while, a song.

Eventually, Dad shied away from singing solos. Not because he couldn't, but the perfectionist in him would not like the output. Even though he still had an unbelievable voice and range, he just didn't sound right to himself. I guess like Jack Nicklaus deciding in his later years not to play ceremonial golf. I think in their minds, doing so would have diminished the level of expertise they had achieved.

I asked him to sing so we could have a CD of some of his favorite songs. He didn't want to at first. Finally, he gave in and did the CD. *Ave Maria* and *Our Father* were on that CD. He sang both of those songs so well that they brought tears to people's eyes, including mine. Those are spiritual songs, of course.

Dad had been a stern disciplinarian, quick to criticize, quick to correct, and sometimes even quick to pass judgment. Looking back, the punches to my arms or the horse bites to my hamstrings when Dad thought I needed correction were his way of showing love and concern for me. Dad remained equally as physical and expressive, only he'd grown to where physical gestures and expressiveness were delivered through hugs and kisses.

In his final years, every conversation ended with an overflow of words of passion, praise, pride, and love.

Coupled with that were Dad's unceasing support and curiosity regarding what was going on in my life. From 2010 to 2012, Skip Holtz—Coach Lou Holtz's son, with whom I'd struck up a friendship during my time at Notre Dame—was the head coach at the

University of South Florida. In the spring of 2011, I got a call from him, and he asked if I wanted to "go and play golf next week." I said, "Sure, where are we playing?" His answer: "A small course up in the corner of Georgia." Though I told him I needed to check my calendar, I immediately responded, "I'm free!"

We laughed because I knew he wasn't talking about some off-the-beaten-path goat track, he was talking about Augusta National. Of course, when I told Dad about my plans for a return trip, he was ecstatic. It was clear he'd be living vicariously through me for this second outing, and he couldn't wait to hear how it went.

Unlike my first trip to the Holy Grail of Golf, this trip took place in the early summer. The course looked just as beautiful and spectacular as it was in the fall of 2003.

The second time around, I had more familiarity of the grounds. That gave me additional confidence when I teed off.

Skip's Dad, Lou, had the Augusta membership, and he brought us together in his room before we went to eat dinner the night before. Dressed in jackets and ties, we listened to Coach Holtz tell us from some scribbled notes in his hand the history and facts of Augusta National.

Listening to Coach Holtz gave me the feeling of being in a time warp. Twenty years earlier, I had listened to Coach Holtz explain the history and facts about Notre Dame as a university and about its football program, noting how much of an honor it was to play or coach at Notre Dame. During this speech, he conveyed the same thing about Augusta National.

As corny as it may sound, he was spot on. Augusta National is the Holy Grail of Golfers. To me, the place stands above all other courses because of its history and what it stands for in the world of golf. Like being at Notre Dame, there are a chosen few every year who get the honor to experience that tradition. I felt privileged and blessed that Coach Holtz and Skip gave me the opportunity to intimately experience both Notre Dame and Augusta National. For that, I am eternally grateful.

When I returned from the trip, Dad had to know every detail about the outing. In fact, Dad might have enjoyed my second trip to Augusta more than I did.

As I recapped the round at Augusta, it was clear from Dad's reaction that I seemed to be some kind of hero to him, though given his veteran status, I always considered heroics more of his thing. Dad visited Arlington National Cemetery for the first time on May 12, 2012, thanks to Honor Flight Southeast Florida, an organization created to help American veterans visit their memorials. He went with a group of eighty-five veterans who were flown up for the one-day trip using the funds raised by the organization that had been created by an Ohio doctor, who had been a soldier and wanted to honor fellow veterans. Dad seemed touched by the visit. The *Miami Laker* wrote a story on his visit, and Dad spoke about the significance of the organization in relation to World War II veterans, noting, "There won't be too many of us left. So now was a good opportunity to go to the memorial and remember those who died for our country."

Remember, Dad never considered himself a hero. He always claimed that the heroes of World War II were the guys who died while fighting for their country.

Speaking of World War II, Dad revealed a little-known part of his life to me when he began to open up to me more.

For most of my life, my relationship with Dad had been one-sided. He'd been stern and anything but open. I wanted my kids to experience more, so I tried to change that with them. I think I've managed to have an open relationship with them. I just don't think Dad was equipped to be open. Still, I never doubted his love for me, which was a good thing, because he sure wasn't going to come out and express his love for me. At least that's the way he was earlier in his life. He made up for being that way later. He identified it in his own shortcomings, and he tried to make up for them. I never asked him about it. I understood it. The more he opened up, I learned things about him I'd never known, like the fact he'd been smitten with an Australian girl when he was in the Navy.

Of course, Dad didn't just reveal the information outright. I gleaned that information from constantly probing him about the war. I asked him about the girls when he was in the Navy. When I asked him, I said, "You were fifteen or sixteen, you were going into these foreign countries, and, well . . ."

He told me he'd met a girl from Australia in a bar on one of the islands where his ship docked. Later, he said he always thought about what she did, how her life turned out, that sort of thing—typical, because we all look back and wonder about the girls we dated. I could tell by his voice he felt as though his life would have been completely different had he married her. Clearly, she had been special to him. After telling me about the girl, he never mentioned her again.

Dad got deeper into his Catholic faith the closer he got to the end of his life. He sang and always stayed involved in the choir. Dad consistently had questions and conversations with the clergy. He was a very inquisitive person, and he was a ferocious reader. Some of his family, and my mom's family, had several priests and nuns in them, and they had friends who were clergy. We always had clergy of some sort around the house and often on Sundays. They were not just religious people; they were friends and family.

He didn't like the movement of the church away from the old Catholic Mass. I remember many conversations on that subject. Dad would question the priests. Most of the time, he'd question them about the changes in the Mass. He remained a traditionalist and liked the old hymns. Naturally, he butted heads with them when they ventured away from that. He got to see the business side of the priesthood, too. Dad felt priests would get too involved where they didn't need to be involved, especially in the music. Many a day he would come home and say, "Those priests don't know what they are talking about!"

Dad had a particular love for Gregorian chant, which is an unaccompanied sacred song of the Roman Catholic Church traditionally performed by choirs of men and boys. Gregorian chant is complicated and has a deep, rich history that dates back to the 9th century.

Dad was so enamored with Gregorian Chant that he once attended a three-day Gregorian chant camp. He said that this was his retreat, his quiet time and a way of praying that brought him closer to his Creator.

Dad died on February 28, 2016.

He never lost his faculties, and his memory was good to the end, unlike that of his deceased brothers and sisters. Prior to Dad's death, all of us were experiencing a tough situation with my mother, who began to lose her memory. She didn't make sense on many occasions and would come home with dings in her car. Trying to get her keys away from her became a big issue.

The relationship my parents had with each other taught me a lot about relationships. They maintained a generally solid relationship, but with two alpha personalities, they had their share of disagreements over the years.

Like many of us, we tell our children how to treat others, then we sometimes fail in the eyes of our kids. My Dad was far from perfect, but he was a playful, loving person to my mother, though definitely not a doting husband. Of course, he would always be quick with a stanza of a song to express his affection. Dad's famous line that he used to sing all the time came from *Camelot*—"How to Handle a Woman," wherein the answer is, of course, simply to love her.

Maybe Dad's memorization of all those Broadway tunes is what kept his mind so sharp all those years!

With both short- and long-term memory still intact, in his later years—up until the day he died, in fact—Dad would consistently bring up the topic of our Augusta outing. I'll forever be grateful to Jack Nicklaus for enabling me to treat Dad to the priceless golf fantasy of a lifetime. I thought about Jack and our special day at Augusta National the day I began composing Louis Joseph Wessel's eulogy.

Not once could I keep it together while writing the tribute that celebrated my father's life. Tears constantly formed when I thought about the man I loved and all that we had shared over the years. But the day of his funeral service at St. Patrick's Catholic Church, I did not shed a tear, and yes, I did sing. I wanted people to know that Solomon would have been proud of Dad. He made life more meaningful than meaningless to so many. He followed God's word as best he could and enjoyed life to its fullest. I also did what he would do by mixing in a tune from several Broadway shows in midsentence. I then ended it like I promised him in my garage twenty-three years earlier—"Lord bring him home so that he can receive the greatest gift exchange in the history of the world, the gift of eternal life." I sang a cappella, asking God to bring him peace, joy, and to his final resting place in Heaven.

An appropriate ending for one's best friend.

Epilogue

THE YEAR FOLLOWING DAD'S DEATH, I didn't play much golf because of a back problem. Most every time I did play, I thought about a conversation we'd had maybe three years prior to his death. I don't know what triggered it, but I told him, "When you get up there, if I get a hole in one, it's got to be a Titleist 1. And if it's staring up at me from the hole, I'll know where you are, and I know you'll be with me." We kind of joked about it. I didn't bring it up a lot, because we didn't have a whole lot of conversations about him dying.

When I did go golfing after he died, I'd make sure when I played a par-3 that I had a Titleist 1 ready to go. I'd take balls out and change it out. For some reason, I wasn't thinking about using a Titleist 1 when I ventured to Oak Hill Country Club in October 2017. I took a group of guys to the famed course in Rochester, New York, that had hosted numerous PGA Tours, U.S. Opens, and even a Ryder Cup. My brother-in-law, Brian Scott, being from Rochester, blessed me many years ago with the privilege of meeting many friends who were members of Oak Hill. I had played Oak Hill many times before and even played in a couple of member-guest tournaments with a great friend, John Post. There was even one time when Joe Huber, who was the best man at my sister Margie's wedding, and I concocted a surprise trip for my dad to play Oak Hill. He did not know that I was going to be the fourth member of the foursome, so I surprised him in the pro shop. That became one of those great father-son moments in my life and remains one of the many reasons why Oak Hill remains a special course for me.

The course would become more special to me after my October 2017 trip, which turned out to be a divine golf trip. We were guests of John Post, who was the current club president.

The East course at Oak Hill is the championship course. We were scheduled to play it twice, on consecutive mornings. But the afternoon round on the West course turned out to be most memorable.

When we teed off, we were the last to do so for our afternoon group.

My foursome included friends Mark O'Conner, Greg Jones, and Greg Iglehart.

My back, which had been a constant source of physical pain for the previous ten years, was giving me fits on that trip. And I wasn't playing well, either. Adding drudgery to the round—if you can possibly call any round at Oak Hill "drudgery"—the greens had just been punched and topdressed. Thus, putting was no easy task.

We approached the 14th tee, a 177-yard par 3 that has a slightly downhill green shaded by trees. I went with a 6-iron and knew I'd hit the ball well. I tracked the ball as best I could. It appeared to be slightly to the right of the flag stick. We knew my ball would be close, but we couldn't see it land. In fact, when we approached the green, we couldn't see any balls on the surface. Suddenly, Greg ran up to the hole and started jumping up and down. "It's in!" he shouted. "It's in! You made a hole in one!"

By this time, the other groups started coming up to the green high-fiving me. In the middle of all the chaos, I pulled a ball out of my pocket and noticed it was a Titleist 3. It then dawned on me that after playing the twelfth hole, I had switched out my Titleist 3 for a Titleist 1. I asked Greg if the logo and the 1 were staring up at him when he pulled it out. He paused briefly and said, "Yes, but why?"

With tears rolling down my face, I struggled for words while recounting the conversation Dad and I had years ago.

I knew where Dad was now! The Titleist 1 gave me that confirmation.

Experiencing better health in October of 2018, I got an opportunity to play at Baltusrol Golf Club, the course where White Fang had been born.

I had first played the historic course in 2005, a week after Phil Mickelson had won the PGA Championship there. My visit on October 11, 2018, came on a golf trip with seven friends from Palma Ceia Golf and Country Club in Tampa. I knew much more about Baltusrol after studying what had happened during the 1967 U.S. Open and had grown more familiar with Jack Nicklaus's victory.

I never got the chance to tour the clubhouse on my first trip, and boy did I miss a lot. The expansive Tudor-looking clubhouse and grounds are among the best that I have seen to date. Walking in the halls and rooms of the clubhouse, I felt as though I were in a golf museum. Trophy cases filled with replicas, clubs, and pictures of champions who had distinguished themselves at Baltusrol (including Mickey Wright, Jack Nicklaus, Kathy Baker, Phil Mickelson, Lee Janzen, and Jimmy Walker, to name a few) were all on display. As I circled around one hallway, I looked to my right, and there was the trophy case that was dedicated to Jack, who won not only the 1967 U.S. Open, but also the 1980 U.S. Open here. Inside that trophy case, I saw a replica of White Fang. The guys with me had heard the story of White Fang over the years. Now, they saw what it looked like.

We had a fabulous dinner, and our sponsor Jeff Bak tried to answer all the questions about Baltusrol and its history. In time, with two bottles of Faust Cabernet empty, the questions shifted to politics, where there were not many answers. Unfortunately, we were not able to stay in the rooms on the property, so we retreated to our hotel.

We teed off under cloudy skies the following morning. The heavy rain held off until the fourteenth, where we headed for shelter and waited. Once the rain stopped, we were able to finish, but we played in wet conditions, including a couple of soaked greens. As we walked down the eighteenth fairway, I couldn't help but think of the story told to me by the Baltusrol historian, Stu Wolffe, to whom I'd been introduced two weeks prior to our trip.

Recall the final round of the 1967 U.S. Open. Nicklaus birdied five of his first eight holes to open up a four-stroke advantage over Arnold Palmer, and that is how they finished. At the par-5 eighteenth, Nicklaus had played safely with a 1-iron off the tee, but it went right and required a recovery shot from the rough. The recovery shot didn't go very far and left him with a 230-yard shot to the green. The third shot was over water and uphill 230 yards from the green. He hit another 1-iron that has been talked about ever since. He then sank the birdie putt from 22 feet for the record score of 275 that stood for thirteen years. Wolffe told me about a man named Larry Carpenter, who had been a marshal stationed on the eighteenth fairway that day. After witnessing Jack's recovery shot, Larry allegedly said, "That was the worst shot I have ever seen." As the story goes, Jack heard the remark, turned around, and quipped, "I agree with you on that!"

Recently, my second cousin John Murphy told me that he and his sister, Marilyn, had attended that very opening round of the 1967 U.S. Open at Baltusrol. John told me they had "gloriously" been a part of Arnie's Army that day. His recount emphasizes what a remarkable round Jack had that day, given the fact that he beat Palmer, who was the 1960 champion, and the turning point marked by that outing.

John recounted the well-known story of Palmer winning the

1960 Masters. While waiting for Arnie to get to the clubhouse, Bobby Jones, arguably the greatest golfer ever, said to Cliff Roberts, the president of Augusta National, "If I had to make a putt, the man I would choose would be Arnold."

"Two years later, the magic was gone," John said. "Arnold lost to Jack in a playoff the 1962 U.S. Open at Oakmont in Pennsylvania. Arnold needed a lot more putts for the four rounds than Jack did.

"Friday of the 1967 U.S. Open, Arnold hit every fairway and every green in regulation. I think he could have shot 62 that day if he'd sunk a few putts. I'm going to my grave believing Arnold was both the greatest sports celebrity and golfer in my lifetime. Arnold smiled and winked at my thirty-seven-year-old sister. She cherished that moment forever."

After Palmer died on September 25, 2016, Jack spoke at his funeral. They had been rivals and friends for decades. During his remarks, Jack said, "[Palmer] was the king of our sport, and he always will be. Like the great [broadcaster] Vin Scully said when he called his last game Sunday night for the Dodgers: 'Don't be sad because it's over. Smile because it happened.' Today I hurt, just like you hurt. You don't lose a friend of over sixty years and not feel an enormous loss. But like my wife always says, 'The memories are the cushions of life.'"

Couldn't have said it better myself, Jack.

We ate lunch after we finished our round at Baltusrol. Before we left the club, a photographer opened the trophy case so we could take pictures of the "White Fang" replica. The original is now housed at the Jack Nicklaus Museum located on the Ohio State University campus in Columbus, Ohio.

Holding the "fake" White Fang (which didn't have a pencil in the handle), I thought about the Golden Bear, Steve Nicklaus, and, of course, Dad. White Fang had brought us all together for an experience of a lifetime.

Appendix

THROUGHOUT, DAD'S WESSELISMS PERMEATED MY life. Here are some of his go-to sayings that he repeated on many occasions, many of which he first delivered when I was a young boy:

"Don't walk off like a goat."
He used this one if I walked away from a job that was undone, or when I walked away from my chores, or if I left a job unfinished.

"I need to go pee on that money tree in the backyard!"
That came when he thought that we wanted him
to buy things that he felt we didn't need.

"Be the best version of yourself."
He basically copied this from Matthew Kelly,
one of the apologists for the Catholic faith.

"New math."
He couldn't understand how people could be spending money on iPhones, cars, etc. Coming from his post-Depression era, he didn't understand how people bought the things that they bought. Even with me, it was his way of questioning my purchases.
He would say, "Must be part of the new math?"

"You drink and I get drunk!"
Dad's go-to line when people would be drinking at dinner,
getting loud, and not making sense.

"You can't fly with the eagles if you're out
with the turkeys all night long."
Obviously, this was when we would come home late.
My parents were great with waking us up early the next day
after we were out late. There were chores to be done. And if
not, they made some up. "Go polish the leaves!"

"You're sandpapering a lion's ass."
This would come when he observed me working on
something, either on the boat or in the garage, and I
wasn't doing it correctly. In essence, I was wasting time,
which he didn't hesitate to point out.

"Don't be a ragamuffin."
This was a reference, and sometimes a term of endearment,
to when we were going out and we had ratty clothes on. He also
would say, "Don't be dressed up like a bag of rags."

"Did someone drop a giffick?"
I don't know where this one stemmed from, but it pertained
to someone passing gas—when something smelled like poop.
I heard Dad deliver this one long before Rodney Dangerfield's
"Somebody step on a duck?"

"Getting old is not for sissies."
Obviously, this one isn't unique to Dad, but later in life,
he often told doctors this during his visits.

"Don't know what you see in that roundball."
Dad's phrase to all of us about basketball. He never quite
understood the attraction of the sport.

"There's no sin if you get knocked down. . . . Sin is not to get up."
Dad never quit. He took an old saying to the next level,
bringing religion into it to make it more meaningful,
which he managed to do a lot of times.

"There is a lot of sadness in the world."
His reaction to a poor golf shot or when there was real tragedy.
Nothing else needed to be said.

Acknowledgments

How does one begin to thank all the people in your life that have helped you become who you are? My fifty-seven years have been filled with far more than I could ever have expected and far more than I deserve.

To my Lord Jesus Christ, without your love and sacrifice, my life would be meaningless. Thanks to my wife, Mary Gayle, who every day shows her love and patience dealing with me. To Trent and Parker, you have given me so much joy in my life. May God bless you with children so you may experience what you have given me. My sisters, Margie and Ann Marie, your love and support have inspired me my whole life. Brian and Scott, you chose to be in this Wessel clan; so glad you did. To Danny, Tricia, Robby, Ryan, Katie, Andrew, and Luke, Papa Joe loved you, and so do I. Papa Joe was the leader of the Wessel band.

A special thanks to my friend and neighbor Ralph Barber, who planted the seed and pushed me to write this book. Thanks to Tris Coburn for representing us on this project. Julie Ganz of Skyhorse Publishing, I can't thank you enough for taking an interest in this story, your patience, and your guidance throughout the project. A special thanks to Mike Parker for recording Papa Joe's Navy experience. Many thanks to Bay Color Photo Lab in Tampa for all your help.

Doug Shields—"Coach"—thanks for making me tell the White Fang story one more time to Bill Chastain.

Bill Chastain—what can I say but thanks, thanks, thanks. Your guidance, patience, and professionalism in taking my thoughts, feelings, and experiences and putting them down on paper is the work of true genius.

To the many coaches and players who have touched my life, thank you for your cushions of life. To the many family members and friends over the years who enriched my life, thank you.

Tuesday a.m. Bible study—what a blessing.

Thanks to all the golfers with whom I have had the pleasure to play and to share this great game we call golf.

This project has reinforced how thankful I am to all US servicemen and servicewomen who never came home from fighting for our freedom. I'm grateful Dad came home.

My sincerest thanks to Jack Nicklaus for his help and for agreeing to write the foreword for this book. You are so much more than the greatest golfer who has ever lived! To my roommate, Steve Nicklaus: two great years at FSU gave us a lifetime of memories. I will always be faster than you.

Last, a big thanks to my mother for her never-ending love and positive outlook throughout my life. This book is a tribute to my dad, but Mom is so very much a heroine in her own right. My sisters will write that one!